A BREATHING AFTER GOD

A BREATHING AFTER GOD

OR, A CHRISTIAN'S DESIRE OF GOD'S PRESENCE

As the hart panteth after the water brooks; so panteth my soul after thee, O God.—PSALM 42:1.

Hide not thine ear at my breathing.
—LAMENTATIONS 3:56.

REV. RICHARD SIBBES

DOCTOR IN DIVINITY, MASTER OF KATHERINE HALL IN
CAMBRIDGE, AND SOMETIME PREACHER OF GRAY'S INN

MINNEAPOLIS

Published by Curiosmith.
Minneapolis, Minnesota.
Internet: curiosmith.com.

The text of the sermon "A Breathing After God" is from: *The Complete Works of Richard Sibbes, D.D.,* Vol. 2, Alexander Balloch Grosart, ed., Edinburgh: James Nichol, 1862.

All footnotes marked "G" are from Alexander B. Grosart.

The Biographical Sketch is from: Erasmus Middleton. *Evangelical Biography; or, an Historical Account of the Lives and Deaths of the Most Eminent and Evangelical Authors and Preachers, etc.* Vol. 3. London: W. Baynes, 1816.

Elizabethan verbs and pronouns are updated to modern English word for word.

The "Guide to the Contents" was added to this edition by the publisher.

ISBN 9781946145444

GUIDE TO THE CONTENTS

Biographical Sketch of

REV. RICHARD SIBBES, D.D.

This grave and solid divine (as Mr. Leigh calls him) was born upon the borders of Suffolk, near Sudbury, and being trained up at school, when he was grown ready for the university, was sent to Cambridge, in 1595, and was admitted into St. John's College, where he so profited in learning, and approved himself by his blameless conversation, that he was promoted from one degree to another in the college; being chosen first scholar, and then fellow of that house. He also took all the degrees of the university, with general approbation and applause. It pleased God to convert him by the ministry of Mr. Paul Baines, whilst he was lecturer at St. Andrew's, in Cambridge. And when Mr. Sibbes had been master of arts some time, he entered into the ministry, and shortly after was chosen lecturer at Trinity Church, in Cambridge: To whose ministry, besides the townsmen, many scholars resorted; so that he became the happy instrument of bringing some souls to GOD, as also of edifying and building up others. He appears, from an archidiaconal register, to have been Vicar of Trinity parish only during the two last years of his life; the famous Dr. Thomas Goodwin having resigned in his favor.

About the year 1625 or 1626, he was chosen master of Katharine-hall in Cambridge, in the government whereof he continued till his dying day; and, like a faithful governor, he was always very careful to procure and advance the good of that little house. For he procured good means and maintenance by his interest in many worthy persons, for the enlargement of the college; and was a means of establishing learned and religious fellows there; insomuch that in his time, it proved a very famous society for piety and learning, both as to fellows and scholars.

But before this, about the year 1618, he was chosen preacher at Gray's Inn, where his ministry found such general approbation and acceptance, that, besides the learned lawyers of the house, many noble personages and many of the gentry and citizens resorted to hear him; and many had reason to bless God for the benefit which they received by him. Dr. William Gouge, who frequently heard him preach, says, "that he sometimes had a little stammering in the time of his preaching, but then his judicious hearers always expected some rare and excellent notion from him."

His learning was mixed with much humility, whereby he was always ready to undervalue his own labors, though others judged them to breathe spirit and life, to be strong of heaven, speaking with authority and power to men's consciences. His care in the course of his ministry was to lay a good foundation in the heads and hearts of his hearers. And though he was a wise master-builder, and that in one of the most eminent auditories for learning and piety which was in the land; yet, according to the grace which was given to him, (which was indeed like that of Elisha, in regard of the other prophets, the elder brother's privilege, a double portion) he was still taking all occasions to preach the fundamentals to them, and, among the rest, the incarnation of the Son of God. And preaching at several times, and by occasion of so many several texts of Scripture concerning this subject, there is scarce any one of those incomparable benefits, which accrue to us thereby, nor any of those holy impressions, which the meditation hereof ought to work in our hearts, which was not by him unfolded. The truth of this appeared so evident to an eminent divine, upon reading his sermons when in print, that he said, "I less wonder now at the noted humility of the author, finding how often his thoughts dwelt upon the humiliation of Christ."

Indeed he was thoroughly studied in the Holy

Scriptures, which made him a man of GOD, *perfect, thoroughly furnished unto every good work;* and, as became a faithful steward of the manifold grace of GOD, he endeavored to teach it to others, and to store them with knowledge, wisdom, and spiritual understanding. He was a man that enjoyed much communion with GOD, and, like John the Baptist, was a burning and shining light, wasting and spending himself to enlighten others.

He was upon all occasions very charitable, drawing forth not only his purse in relieving, but his very bowels in commiserating, the wants and necessities of the poor members of Christ. He used sometimes, in the summertime, to go abroad to the houses of some worthy personages, where he was an instrument of much good, not only by his private labors, but by his prudent counsel and advice, that upon every occasion he was ready to minister unto them. And thus having done his work on earth, he was received to heaven, peaceably and comfortably resigning up his spirit unto GOD, in the year 1635, and in the fifty-eighth year of his age.

HIS WORKS. He was "famous (says Mr. Leigh) for the piety, learning, devotion, and politeness [he means polished style] of his two genuine writings, *The Bruised Reed*, and *The Souls Conflict.*" These we have seen, and can assure the Christian reader, who is under exercise of spirit, that he will hardly be able to find two books written by man, which are more likely to afford him direction, comfort, and relief, than these most excellent pieces of Dr. Sibbes. We regret that they are out of print; or rather, that the piety of the times does not hasten them into print again. Upon the subject of spiritual distress, there is scarce any book in our language more valuable, except the Bible. At least, the writer has found it so respecting himself. His "Divine Meditations and Holy Contemplations," were reprinted in 1775, in a small duodecimo,[1] dedicated to the Countess of Huntingdon, and recommended by the honorable and reverend Mr. Walter Shirley. His Sermons on Canticles 5 are so excellent, that the judicious Mr. John Dod, having perused them in manuscript, would not cease soliciting Dr. Sibbes till he had prevailed upon him to print them; and for that end wrote to him as follows: "——I judge it altogether unmeet, (says he) that such precious matter should be concealed from the public use. I judge these Sermons a very profitable and excellent help, both to the understanding of that dark and most divine Scripture, as also to kindle in the heart all heavenly affections towards Jesus Christ: The whole frame whereof is carried with such wisdom, gravity, piety, judgment, and experience, that it commends itself to all that are godly wise: And I doubt not but they shall find their temptations answered, their fainting

---

1 Duodecimo—a book in which a sheet is folded into twelve leaves. *(Webster's 1828 Dictionary)*

spirits revived, their understandings enlightened, and their graces confirmed; so that they shall have cause to praise God for the worthy Author's godly and painful labors."

TO THE CHRISTIAN READER

Man in this world, especially since his defection from God, standing at a distance from his happiness in respect of full possession, it is not the least part of his bliss to be happy in expectation. Happiness being by all men desirable, the desire of it is naturally engrafted in every man; and is the center of all the searchings of his heart and turnings of his life. But the most of men, like the men of Sodom, grope and find not the right door.[1] Only to a true Christian, by a supernatural light, is discovered both the right object, and the right way to felicity. Upon this discovery, finding himself, while he is here, a stranger to his happiness, he desires to take leave of this sublunary condition, that he may enjoy him who is the "desire of all nations."[2]

Now although God cast common blessings

1 Genesis 19:11.
2 Haggai 2:7.

promiscuously upon good and bad; yet he holds his best favors at a distance, as parents do cherries or apples from their children, to whet their appetites the more after them. And indeed the best perfection of a Christian in his military[1] condition, is, in desire and expectation; and it is enough to him that; for that he has God's acceptation, who knowing whereof we are made, and to how unable to hold weight in the "balance of the sanctuary,"[2] takes his best gold with grains of allowance.

The soul of man is like a cipher, which is valued by that which is set before it. If it weary itself in the desire of earthly things, like the silk-worm, it finishes its work with its own destruction. But if on things above, when this earthly tabernacle is turned to ashes, there shall result a glorious phoenix for immortality.

There are no characters better distinguishing a Christian, than those that are inward (hypocrisy like sale-work, may make a fair show outward; an hypocrite may perform external works, but cannot dissemble inward affections), and amongst them, none better discovers his temper, than the beating of the pulse of his desires, which this worthy author (who departed not without being much desired[3] and no less lamented) has most livelily set forth in

---

1 That is "militant."—G.

2 Daniel 5:27.

3 That is, "longed after."—G

the ensuing treatise; which a Christian, holding as a glass before him, may discern whether he have life or no by these breathings.

For the object here propounded, what more desirable than the chief good? For the place, where can it be more desired, than in his house, where his presence is manifested? What better end to be in that house, than to behold God in the "beauty of holiness?"[1] What term of happiness better than "for ever"? This was the desire of the holy prophet David, and that it may be thy desire, is the desire of

Thy Christian friend,

H. I.[2]

---

1 Psalm 29:2.
2 These initials are in all probability those of John Hill, reversed, intentionally or by a misprint.—G.

A BREATHING AFTER GOD

by Richard Sibbes, D.D.

*One thing have I desired of the Lord, that I will
seek after; that I may dwell in the house of the Lord
all the days of my life; to behold the beauty of the
Lord, and to inquire in his temple.*—PSALM 27:4.

This psalm is partly a prophecy. It was made
after some great deliverance out of some
great trouble. The blessed prophet David,
having experience of God's goodness suitable to the
trouble he was in, in the first part of this excellent
psalm he shows—

I. His *comfort;* and, II. His *courage;* and, III.
His care.

I. His *comfort.* It was altogether *in the Lord,*
whom he sets out in all the beauties and excellency
of speech he can. He propounds the Lord to him
in borrowed terms. "The Lord is my light and my
salvation, the strength of my life."[1] So he fetches

1 Psalm 27:1.

comfort from God, the spring of comfort, the "Father of all comfort."[1] He labors to present God to him in the sweetest manner that may be. He opposes him to every difficulty and distress. In darkness, he is "my light"; in danger, he is "my salvation"; in weakness, he is "my strength"; in all my afflictions and straits, he is the "strength of my life." Here is the art of faith in all perplexities whatsoever, to be able to set somewhat in God against every malady in ourselves. And this is not simply set out, but likewise with a holy insultation.[2] "The Lord is my light and salvation; whom shall I fear?"[3] It is a question proceeding from a holy insultation, and daring of all other things. "The Lord is the strength of my life; of whom shall I be afraid?" That is one branch of his comfort.

The second branch and ground of his comfort is, 2. *The goodness of God in the ruin and destruction of his enemies.* "When the wicked, even mine enemies and foes, came upon me to eat up my flesh, they stumbled and fell."[4] He describes his enemies by their malice, and by their ruin.

[1.] His enemies were *cruel enemies*, bloodsuckers, eaters of flesh. We call them cannibals. As indeed men that have not grace, if they

---

1 2 Corinthians 1:4.
2 That is, "defiance."—G.
3 Psalm 27:1.
4 Psalm 27:2.

have greatness, and be opposed, their greatness is inaccessible; one man is a devil to another. The Scripture calls them "wolves, that leave nothing till morning."[1] As the great fishes eat up the little ones, so great men they make no more conscience of eating up other men, than of eating bread; they make no more bones of overthrowing men and undoing them, than of eating bread. "They eat up my people as they eat bread."[2]

[2.] But notwithstanding their cruelty, *they were overthrown.* Says David, "when my foes came upon me to eat up my flesh, they stumbled and fell." For, indeed, God's children, when they are delivered, it is usually with the confusion of their enemies. God does two things at once, because the special grievance of God's children it is from inward and outward enemies. He seldom or never delivers them but with the confusion of their enemies. So he sets down his own comfort in the Lord, by the confusion of his enemies. This will be most apparent at the day of judgment, when Satan, and all that are led by his spirit, all the malignant church, shall be sent to their own place, and the church shall be for ever free from all kind of enemies. When the church is most free, then the enemies of the church are nearest to destruction; like a pair of balances, when they are up at the one end, they are down at

1 Zephaniah 3:3.
2 Psalm 27:2.

the other. So when it is up with the church, down go the enemies. So here are the two branches of his comfort.

II. Now his *courage* for the time to come, that is, in the third verse. "Though an host encamp against me, my heart shall not fear." He puts the case of the greatest danger that can be. Though an host of men should encompass me, "my heart shall not fear; though war rise against me, in this I will be confident." Here is great courage for the time to come. *Experience breeds hope and confidence.* David was not so courageous a man of himself; but upon experience of God's former comfort and assistance, his faith brake as fire out of the smoke, or as the sun out of a cloud. Though I was in such and such perplexities, yet for the time to come I have such confidence and experience of God's goodness, that I will not fear. He that sees God by a spirit of faith in his greatness and power, he sees all other things below as nothing. Therefore he says here, he cares not for the time to come for any opposition; no, not of an army. "If God be with us, who can be against us?"[1] He saw God in his power; and then, looking from God to the creature, alas! who was he? As Micah, when he had seen God sitting upon his throne; what was Ahab to him, when he had seen God once? So when the prophet David had seen God once, then "though an host encamp against

1 Romans 8:31.

me, I will not fear," etc. Thus you have his comfort in the double branch of it; his courage, also, and his confidence for the time to come.

III. What is his *care?* That is the next. I will not analyze the psalm farther than the text. After his comfort in the Lord, and in the confusion of his enemies, and his courage for the time to come, he sets down his care, "One thing have I desired of the Lord, and that will I seek after, that I may dwell in the house of the Lord all the days of my life," etc. This was his care. He had so sweet experience of the goodness and power of God, being light, and salvation and strength to him in confounding his enemies, that he studied with himself how to be thankful to God; and this he thought fittest in the open great congregation, in the church of God, among many others. Therefore he says, "One thing have I desired of the Lord, and that will I seek after still, that I may dwell in the house of the Lord all the days of my life."

Now, in the words of the text that I have read, there is contained the holy prophet's care and desire, set down first in general, "One thing have I desired of the Lord, and that I will seek after."

And then a specification of that desire he specifies. What is that one thing he desired? That "I may dwell in the house of the Lord," with the circumstance of time, "all the days of my life."

Now, after the desire in general, set out here by

the object in general, the transcendent object, "One thing have I desired of the Lord," and likewise by the frequency and fervency of the desire, "I will seek after it still." I have desired it, and I will not cease. So my desire, it shall not be a flash soon kindled, and soon put out. No; but "one thing have I desired of the Lord, and that I will seek still." I will not be quiet till my desire be accomplished. There is the general desire, and the degrees of it.

The particular is, "that I may dwell in the house of the Lord."

Then the grounds and ends of the particular desire of dwelling in the "house of the Lord," because it is "the house of God." There is a strong argument to move him to dwell in the house of God. It is good dwelling where God dwells, where his angels dwell, and where his Spirit dwells, "in the house of the Lord." There is one argument that moved him, "I desire to dwell there," because it is the house of God, which is set out by the extent of time, that "I may dwell in the house of God all the days of my life," till I be housed in heaven, where I shall need none of these ordinances that I stand in need of in this world. "I desire to dwell in the house of the Lord all the days of my life."

Then the second end is, "To behold the beauty of God." That was one end of his desire, to dwell in the house of God; not to feed his eyes with specula-tions and goodly sights (as indeed there were in the tabernacle goodly things to be seen). No; he had a more spiritual sight than that. He saw the inward spiritual beauty of those spiritual things. The other were but outward things, as the apostle calls them. I desire to dwell in the house of the Lord, "to behold the beauty of the Lord," the inward beauty of the Lord especially.

And then the third end of his desire is, "that I may inquire in his temple." He desired to dwell in the house of God, because it was the house of God, and to see the beauty of God, the sweet, alluring beauty of God, that appeared in his ordinances; and then his desire was to dwell in the house of God, that he might inquire more and more of the meaning of God still, because there is an unfathomed bottom, and an endless depth of excellency in divine things, that the more we know, the more we may, and the more we seek, the more we may seek. They are beyond our capacity; they do not only satisfy, but transcend it. Therefore, he desires still further and further to wade deeper into these things, "to inquire in God's temple." Thus you see the state of the verse. There is a general desire propounded. "One thing have I desired of the Lord, and that will I seek after."

And then the desire specified, "to dwell in the house of the Lord, and to see the beauty of the Lord, and to inquire in his temple." These be the three ends.

"One thing have I desired of the Lord," etc.

To speak first of this desire generally propounded, "One thing have I desired," etc.

And then of the increase of it, in that he says, "I will seek after it still." He desired it, and he would seek more and more after it. In the desire, consider—

First, the *object*, "one thing."

And then the *desire* or *seeking itself.*

First, the *object*, "one thing."

QUESTION 1. Was there but one thing for holy David to make the object of his desire? Was there but one thing needful? Alas! this poor life of ours, it is a life of necessities. How many things are needful for our bodies? How many things are needful for the decency of our condition? How many things need we for our souls? It is a life of necessities. How, then, does he say, "One thing have I desired?"

ANSWER 1. Yes. His meaning is, comparatively, I seek for other things in their order and rank, and as they may stand with the main; but, indeed, one thing principally. All the rest will follow. "Seek ye first the kingdom of God, and all the rest will be cast on you."[1] The best way to have all other things, is to seek one thing in the first place. Therefore, in heavenly wisdom he says, I desire *unum unicè;* one thing after an entire manner. That I desire more than all things else.

1 Matthew 6:33.

Hence we may see that,

There is a difference of degrees of things. God has established in the world degrees of things. There are some good and some ill by his permission; and of good, there are some that are greater goods, and some less. There are spiritual goods, and outward goods; and of spiritual good, there are some that are means leading to that which is spiritually good, and some that are spiritual good things in their own essence and nature. The leading preparing things are the means of salvation, the Word, and sacraments, and being in the visible church. The true spiritual good, the good that we get by these things, faith and love, and spiritual inward strength. Now that there is degrees of things, the prophet here insinuates when he says, "One thing have I desired"; that is, of all these variety of things, he desired the best, that includes all in it. God, to exercise the wisdom that he has given to man, has planted a difference in the creatures, and has given a faculty to man to make a right choice in those differences; and then man makes a right choice when he chooses as God chooses. Now, God makes choice of spiritual things to be the best things, and them he gives to his best friends. He knows they will make us good, and supply all outward wants whatsoever, and sanctify all estates and conditions to us, and they are eternal, suitable to the spiritual nature of our souls. God knows this very well. Therefore, God has set spiritual things, as the one only thing; and so the soul, when it is made spiritual, and has the image of God upon it, it chooses as God chooses.

"One thing have I desired."

QUESTION 2. But here it may be asked, why does he say, "one thing?" He desired not only to live near the tabernacle, but to hear and see, to have the Word read, and he desired thereupon grace, and then nearer communion with God by grace, to have more communion here, and fuller communion in heaven. Here is more than one thing.

ANSWER 2. I answer, it is all one. As a chain that has many links, yet it is but one chain; so all these are but one. "I desire one thing." What is that? To live in the church of God, to enjoy the ordinances of God, and they will draw on faith and fear, etc. The Spirit accompanying the ordinances, it will be a spirit of faith, and repentance, and grace; and by those graces of faith, and the rest that accompany the ordinances, I shall have nearer communion with God here, and eternal and everlasting communion with God in heaven; and all these are but one, because they are all links of one chain. Therefore, when he says, "One thing have I desired," he means that one thing that will draw on all other.

That is the scope of a gracious heart, when it attends upon the means of salvation, and lives in the church; not to hear that it may hear, and there an end, and to read that it may read, to perform it as a task, and all is done; but to have the work of the Spirit together with it, to have the ministry of the Spirit in the gospel, and the Spirit to increase faith, and faith to increase all other graces, and so by grace to grow into nearer communion with God in Christ. That is the scope of every good hearer. Therefore, he speaks to purpose when he says, "One thing have I desired."

But to speak a little more of the object, why does he say, "One thing?"

FIRST, *it is from the nature of God.* We must have the whole bent and sway of our souls to him. He will have no halting. The devil is content with half, if we will sin, because then he is sure of all; but God will have the whole heart. "My son, give me thy whole heart,"[1] and "Thou shalt love the Lord with all thy heart, and with all thy soul."[2] The bent and sway of the soul must be that way; for it is the nature of excellent things, except we desire them in the chief place, they take state upon them.[3] God takes state upon him in this case. He will not have us serve him and Mammon.[4] He will not have the heart divided.

SECOND. Then again, *it is from the nature of the soul.* Therefore, he says, "One thing." It is the

---

1 Proverbs 23:26.

2 Luke 10:27.

3 That is, "are offended."—G.

4 Matthew 6:24.

nature of the soul, when it is upon many things, it can do nothing well. Therefore, that I may be religious to purpose, "One thing have I desired." A stream cut into many channels runs weakly, and is unfit to carry anything. Babylon was so taken. They cut the river into many channels, and then he that took it easily passed over them. (*a.*) When the soul is divided into many channels, to many things, that it looks after this thing and that thing, and that with expense and intention of care and endeavor, alas! where is the desire of one thing necessary all the while? For the soul cannot go with that strength as it should, except it mind one thing. The soul of man is a finite thing. Therefore, except it gather its strength, as a stream, that rises of many particular lesser rivers, which makes it run stronger; so the soul it cannot desire one thing as it should, except it bring all other petty streams to it, and make that the main desire, to be saved in another world, and to have communion and fellowship with God in Christ Jesus, by the Spirit of grace in this world, in the use of the means. Unless this be the main care, the soul takes no good when it is so much set on other things.

Then, THIRDLY, he sets down this "one thing," to "dwell in the house of God," to grow in grace there "as a cedar," to be "a tree planted there," *from the very nature of grace,* which is to unite things to the main. The Spirit of grace sets before the eye

of the soul heavenly spiritual things in their greatness and excellency; and the Spirit of grace, seeing there are many useful things in this world, it
has an uniting, knitting, subordinating power, to
rank all things so as they may agree to and help the
main. Grace confines the soul to one thing. Man,
after his fall, "sought out many inventions,"[1] says
the wise man. He was not content with his condition when he stood, but he sought out many inventions. When man falls to the creature, he knows not
where to stay. No creature can afford a stay and rest
for the soul long. The soul is never quiet till it come
to God again,[2] and that is the one thing the soul
desires. The soul being sanctified by the Spirit of
God, it subordinates all things to this one thing.
David desired many things besides this one thing,
but not in that degree, but as they might stand with
the desire of this one thing necessary. Grace subordinates and ranks all things so as that the best
things have the preeminence. Therefore, he might
well say, "one thing," from the disposition that
grace has to rank all things to one. It is a promise
in the covenant of grace. Says God, "I will give you
one heart."[3] As soon as a man becomes a Christian,
he has "one heart." His heart before was divided.
There was variety of objects it was set upon; God

---

1 Ecclesiastes 7:29.

2 Augustine.—G.

3 Jeremiah 32:39.

had the least piece. The flesh had a piece, and this delight and that delight had a piece; but says God, "I will give you one heart," that is, a heart uniting itself in desire to the best things, and regulating all things, so as all shall be but one, that a man shall "use the world as though he used it not," so as it shall help to the main. As I said, little streams they help the main stream running into it, so grace has a subordinating power over all things in the world, as they may help the main. "One thing have I desired," and I desire other things, as they may help the main. Grace will teach us that art. It has a special art that way. So we see both in regard of God, and in regard of the soul being finite, and in respect of the wise disposing of grace that aims at the main, and ranks all things as they may help the main, he does well say, "One thing have I desired."

USE. This shows *the vanity and baseness of every worldly man, that makes the main work and labor his by-work, and the by-work his main work.* That that is the "one thing necessary,"[1] is set after all. Indeed, without grace, this is so. The first work of grace is to set the soul in order, to subdue base affections, to sanctify the judgment; and when it has set the soul in tune and order, then it is fitted to set a right price on things, to rank and order them as it should. So much shall be sufficient to unfold the object itself in general, "One thing have I desired."

1 Luke 10:42.

Now I come to the affection itself, set forth here by the degrees.

"One thing have I desired, *and that I will seek after.*"

I have desired it, and I will desire it still. Desires are the issues of the heart. Thoughts and desires are the two primitive issues of the heart, the births of the heart. Thoughts breed desires. Thoughts in the mind or brain, the brain strikes the heart presently. It goes from the understanding to the will and affections. What we think of, that we desire, if it be good. So thoughts and desires, they immediately spring from the soul; and where they are in any efficacy and strength, they stir up motion in the outward man. The desires of the soul, being the inward motion, they stir up outward motion, till there be an attaining of the thing desired, and then there is rest. Desire to the thing desired is like *motus ad quietem*, as motion is to rest. When motion comes once to rest, it is quiet. So desire, which is the inward motion, it stirs up outward motion, till the thing desired be accomplished, and then the soul rests in a loving content, and enjoying of the thing desired.

Now this desire, it was a spiritual desire. "One thing have I desired of the Lord." Holy desires, they issue from choice. A holy, wise desire, when it is not a mere notion, it arises from a choice of a thing that is good; for desire is nothing but the embracing and closing with a thing that is good. The under-standing must choose the good first, before the soul embrace it. The will is but the carriage of the soul, the furthering and promotion of the soul to the good things discovered; so it supposes a choice of good things.

And choice supposes an esteem of the things before we choose them; and that supposes a delib-erate judging that works an esteem. So that it was no hasty, sudden thing this desire; but it rose from the sanctified judgment of David, that bred a holy esteem of these excellent things; the means of sal-vation, having the Spirit of God accompanying of them, containing such excellent comforts as they do. I say this desire supposes a right judgment, and thence an esteem; thence a choice upon all, choos-ing these things above all other contentments and things in the world besides. For at this time he wanted in his family the comfort of his wife and house, etc. Tush, what do I regard these things? If I could enjoy the sweet, and strong, and comfortable presence of God in his ordinances, other things I could bear well enough, the want of house, and wife and children, the pleasures and contentments of my country. Therefore, "One thing have I desired." It was a desire out of a high esteem and choice of that one thing he speaks of.

The point of doctrine that I will observe in brief, because I hasten to the main thing, is this,

That the Spirit of God in the hearts of his children is effectual in stirring up holy desires.

There is nothing that characterizes and sets a stamp upon a Christian so much as desires. All other things may be counterfeit. Words and actions may be counterfeit, but the desires and affections cannot, because they are the immediate issues and productions of the soul; they are that that comes immediately from the soul, as fire cannot be counterfeit. A man may ask his desires what he is? According to the pulse of the desires, so is the temper of the man. Desires are better than actions a great deal; for a man may do a good action, that he does not love, and he may abstain from an ill action, that he hates not. But God is a Spirit, and looks to the spirit especially. It is a good character of a Christian, that his desire, for the most part, is to good; the tenor and sway and bent of his desire is to good. "One thing have I desired." The Spirit of God is effectual in stirring up these desires.

QUESTION 1. But how shall we know that these desires are the chief things to distinguish an hypocrite from a true Christian, and whether they be true or no?

ANSWER 1. To go no farther than the text: desires are holy and spiritual,

If they be about holy and spiritual things. "One thing have I desired," says David. What was that? To be rich and great in the world, and to be revenged on my enemies? No, no; that is not the matter. I have many enemies; God will take a course that they shall fall. That that I desire, is to have nearer communion with God; I desire to enjoy the ordinances of God. So his desire it was set on spiritual objects, and that argued it was a holy desire.

2. And then again, his desire. It was a *fervent desire,* as he says, "One thing have I desired, and that will I seek after." It was not a blaze or flash, that was soon in and soon out. It was not a mere velleity, a kind of inefficacious desire. Fervency showed that his desire was sound. He would not be quieted without the thing accomplished.

3. And then *constancy*, when a man will not be taken off. There is not the wickedest man in the world, but he has good flashes, good offers, and desires sometimes. "Lord, have mercy upon me," etc. He has good ejaculations sometimes. Ay, but what is the bent and sway of his desires? This was David's constant desire. As it was about spiritual, and was a fervent and eager desire, that he would not be quieted, so it was constant. That that is natural is constant, and that that is supernaturally natural. That that is natural in spiritual things, it is constant; nature is constant. For how does nature differ from art? Artificial things are for a time. Teach a creature beyond his nature, he will show his naturals. So let an hypocrite act a part, if it be not his nature, he will soon turn to his naturals, and

show that he is an hypocrite again. Constancy and perpetuity in good things, a tenor of good desires, show that the heart is good, because it is constant.

4. And then again, this desire here, of David, it was kindled *from the love of God, and not out of base ends.* Holy desires are kindled in the soul from the love of God; for what says he here? "One thing have I desired." What was that? "To dwell in the house of the Lord." What to do? "To behold the beauty of God;" to see God in his excellency and beauty and worthiness. All his desire was from this, that his soul was enamored with the beauty of God's house. The love of God stirred up this blessed desire in the prophet. Therefore, it was a holy and spiritual desire.

5. Again, as they spring from the love of God, *so they tend to the honor of God;* for what comes from heaven, goes to heaven back again. As waters that come from a spring, they go as high as the place they come from; so holy desires, being kindled from heaven from a spirit of love, they go to heaven again. The love of God stirs them up, and he seeks God's glory, and honor, and inward communion with God in this. For a man out of a natural desire may desire holy things sometimes, to be free from such or such a sin, and to have such and such a grace, not out of a desire to honor God; but if he had grace, he sees he might escape troubles, he might be free from temporal judgments, and he

might ingratiate himself, and commend himself to this or that person, whom he desires to benefit by. Therefore, he desires as much grace as may help forward his intentions in the world. He joins the world and God together. Oh! no, these are not the desires that distinguish a Christian from another man; but those that spring from the love of God, that proceed inwardly from the truth of the heart, and that the things themselves please God, and that there is a loveliness in them, and that they tend to the honor of God especially, and our own good in a secondary place. This is a character of good desires. Thus we see, though I should go no further than the text, how we may distinguish holy and heavenly desires from other desires. "One thing have I desired, and that will I seek," etc.

Therefore, let us examine what our desires are, what our bent is. Desires issue from the will and affections, and they show the frame of the soul more than anything in the world. As the springs in low places are discovered by the steams and vapors that come out of the place, men gather that there is a spring below, because of the ascent of vapors; so the vaporing out of these desires show that there is a spring of grace in the heart; they discover that there is a spring within.

And let those that mourn in Sion, that have some evidence (though they are not so good as they would be), let them look to their hearts. What is your desire? What is the bent of your soul? When a man is once converted and turned, wherein is his turning? Especially, his mind and judgment and esteem of things are altered. There is a change of mind, and withal the desire and bent of the soul is altered; that if a man ask him, and examine what the bent is of all the course of his life, oh! that God might be glorified, that his church and cause might prosper, that others might be converted; this is the bent of his soul; not that he might be great in the world, and ruin those that stand in his way (this shows that a man is a rotten hypocrite). The bent and sway of the soul shows what a man is.

Because I would not have any deceived in the point, take one evidence and sign more with you, and that shall be instead of all, and it is out of the text too, "One thing have I desired, and that will I seek after," not by prayer only, but in the use of all means; as, indeed, he was never quiet till he was settled again in Sion, nor then neither till he had gotten materials for the temple, and a place for God's honor "to dwell in."[1] If desires be not the desires of the sluggard, there will be endeavor; as we see in the desire of David here, "One thing have I desired, and that will I seek." He used all means to enjoy communion with God sweetly.

The sluggard lusts and has nothing. So there are many spiritual sluggards that lust and have nothing,

1 Deuteronomy 12:11.

because they show not their desire in their endeavors. There will be endeavor where the desire is true. For desire springs from the will, the will being the appetite of the whole man, *Voluntas appetitus*, etc. The understanding carries not, but the will. When the will will have a thing, it carries all the parts. Hereupon, when the desire is true, it stirs up all the powers and faculties to do their duty, to seek to attain the accomplishment and possession of that that is desired.

Those, therefore, that pretend they have good desires to God, and yet live scandalously and negligently, and will take no pains with their souls, alas! it is the sluggard's desire, if they take not pains to remove all lets and hindrances. For a man may know the desire of a thing is good when he labors to set the hindrances out of the way, if he can. If the lets and hindrances be not impossible, he will remove it, if he can. Therefore, those that pretend this and that, "There is a lion in the way,"[1] when they might remove it, if they would, there is no true desire; for desire is with the removing of all possible hindrances of the thing desired.

QUESTION 2. But to resolve one question. How shall I know whether my desire be strong enough and ripe enough or no to give me comfort?

ANSWER 2. I answer, if the desire of grace *be above the desire of any earthly thing*, that a man

1 Proverbs 26:13.

may say with David, "One thing have I desired," I desire to be free from sin, as a greater blessing to my soul, than to be free from any calamity, Oh! it is a good sign. And surely a man can never have comfort of his desire till his desires be raised to that pitch. For none ever shall come to heaven that do not desire the things that tend to heaven, above all earthly things; nor none shall ever escape hell that do not think it worse and more terrible than all earthly miseries. God brings no fools to heaven that cannot discern the difference of things. Therefore, let us know, that our desires are to little purpose if we have some desire to be good, etc.; but we have a greater desire to be rich and great in the world, to have such and such place. If the desire of that be greater than to be gracious with God, if we hate poverty, and disgrace, and want, and this and that more than sin and hell, to which sin leads, it is a sign that our judgments are rotten and corrupt, and that our desire is no pure spiritual desire. For it is not answerable to the thing desired; there is no proportion. David says here, "One thing have I desired." His desire carried him amain to "one thing necessary," above all other things whatsoever. Thus you see out of the text, what are the distinguishing notes of true desires from those that are false. I need name no more, if we consider what has been spoken.

Now for our comfort, if we find these holy

desires: Oh! let us take comfort in ourselves: for "God will fulfil the desires of them that fear him."[1] Holy desires, they are the birth of God's Spirit, and there is not one of them that shall be lost; for God regards those desires, "My groanings are not hid from thee,"[2] my groanings in trouble, and desires of grace. There is not the least thing stirred up in the soul by the Spirit of God, but it prevails with God in some degree, answerable to the degree of worth in it. Therefore, if we have holy desires stirred up by God, God promotes those desires. God will regard his own work, and to "him that has shall be given."[3] "Lord, be merciful to thy servants, that desire to fear thy name," says Nehemiah 1:11.[4] It is a plea that we may bring to God, "Lord, I desire to please thee," as it is, "The desire of our souls is to thy name, O Lord."[5] We fail sometimes, that we cannot perform actions with that zeal and earnestness as we should; but the desire and bent of our soul is to thy name. A Christian may make it his plea to God—truly our desires are towards thy name, and we have some suitable endeavors; and our desires are more that way than to anything in the world. It is a good plea, though we be much hindered and pulled back by

---

1 Psalm 37:4.
2 Psalm 37:9.
3 Matthew 13:12.
4 Misprinted "Ezechias"= Hezekiah.—G.
5 Isaiah 27:8.

our corruptions. So much for that, the act upon this object, "One thing have I desired."

Of whom does he desire it? Of the Lord.

"One thing have I desired of the Lord."

It was not a blind desire of the thing, *but a desire directed to the right object, to God*, to fulfil it. Holy desires are such as we are not ashamed of, but dare open them to God himself in prayer, and desires to God. A Christian, what he desires as a Christian, he prays for, and what he prays for he desires; he is a hypocrite else. If a man pray, as St. Austin, in his confessions,[1] that God would free him from temptations, and yet is unwilling to have those loving baits from him, he prays, but he does not desire. There are many that pray; they say in their prayers, "Lead us not into temptation,"[2] and yet they run into temptation; they feed their eyes, and ears, and senses with vain things. You know what they are well enough, their lives are nothing but a satisfying of their lusts, and yet they pray, "Lead us not in temptation." And there are many persons that desire that, that they dare not pray for, they desire to be so bad. But a Christian what he desires, he prays for. I desire in earnest to be in the house of the Lord, I desire it of the Lord, I put up my request to him; and what I pray to him for, I earnestly desire

1 Conf. A reminiscence rather than translation, of a recurring sentiment in the "Confessions."—G.

2 Matthew 6:13.

indeed. Learn this in a word, hence, that,

When we have holy desires stirred up by God, turn them to prayers.

A prayer is more than a desire. It is a desire put up to God. Let us turn our desires into prayers. That is the way to have them speed.

"One thing have I desired of the Lord."

The reason why we should, in all our desires, make our desires known to God, is to keep our acquaintance continually with God. We have continual use of desires of grace, and desires of mortification of corruptions, and of freedom from this and that evil that is upon us. As many desires as we have, let them be so many prayers; turn our desires into prayers to God, and so maintain our acquaintance with God. And we shall never come from God without a blessing and comfort. He never sends any out of his presence empty, that come with a gracious heart, that know what they desire. And it brings peace with it, when we make our desires known to God by our prayer. It brings "peace that passeth understanding."[1] Put case God does not hear our request, that he does not grant what we ask. "The peace of God which passes understanding, shall keep your hearts and minds." So that when we put up our requests to God with thankfulness for what we have received, the soul will find peace. Therefore I say, let us turn all our

1 Philippians 4:7.

desires into prayers, to maintain perpetual communion and acquaintance with God. Oh! it is a gainful and comfortable acquaintance.

It is an argument, and sign of a good conscience, for a man to go oft to God with his desires. It is a sign that he is not in a wicked course; for then he dares not appeal to the presence of God. Sore eyes cannot endure the light; and a galled conscience cannot endure God's presence. Therefore it is good to come oft into the presence of God. It shows that the heart does not regard iniquity. "If I regard iniquity in my heart, God will not hear my prayers."[1] It is an argument of a good conscience to come oft into the presence of God. But I will not enter into the common place of prayer.

We see next his earnestness, "I have desired it of the Lord, *and I will seek after it.*"

I will follow God still. Here is his importunity in prayer, his fervency, his uncessancy and perseverance, as the apostle exhorts, he persevered in prayer, "I will seek after it."[2] In prayer, and in the use of all good means, I will do what I can. So you see one qualification of prayer, *it must be with perseverance and importunity.* God loves importunate suitors. Though we cannot endure to be troubled with such persons, yet God loves importunate suitors, as we see in Luke 18:1–8, in the parable of the widow.

1 Psalm 66:18.
2 Ephesians 6:18.

God there vouchsafes to compare himself to an unrighteous judge, that "cared neither for God nor man," yet the importunity of the widow moved him to regard her. So the poor church of God, she is like a widow, with her hair hanging about her. "This is Zion, whom none regardeth;" yet this widow, the poor church of God, and every particular member of it, they are importunate with the Judge of heaven and earth, with God; and will not he more regard the importunity of his children whom he loves, and delights in, that "call upon him day and night"?[1] will not he regard their petitions, when an unrighteous judge shall care for the importunity of a poor widow? Thus you see the excellent fruit of importunity in our blessed Saviour himself, and here in David, "I will seek after it," I will have no nay. Therefore we are exhorted in the Scriptures, not to keep silence, to give God no rest. "You that are the Lord's remembrancers, keep not silence, give him no rest." As Jacob with the angel, wrestle with him, leave him not till we have a blessing. As the woman of Canaan, let us follow him still, and take no nay. Oh this is a blessed violence, beloved, when we can set upon God, and will have no nay, but renew suit upon suit, and desire on desire, and never leave till our petitions be answered. Can the hypocrite pray always? Would you know a comfortable note to distinguish an hypocrite from a true Christian? take it

1 Psalm 102:2.

hence, will the hypocrite pray always? Sometimes he will pray; but if God answer him not presently he gives over; but God's children pray always, if the ground be good, if they see the excellency of the thing, and the necessity, and withal join at the amiableness of it, that it may be gotten. When they see the excellency, and the necessity and usefulness of the thing, and the attainableness of it, and that it is attainable in the use of means, they need no more, they will never give over. That is the reason of that in the petitions, "kingdom come, thy will be done in earth as it is in heaven."[1] But can we do the will of God on earth as it is done in heaven? and does God's glorious kingdom of heaven come while we are here on earth? No; it does not, but the soul that is guided with the spirit of prayer, it rests not in this or that degree, but prays till it be in heaven, "Thy kingdom come." I have grace now, but I desire glory. "Thy will be done." I desire to do it as thy saints in heaven, though I cannot do it; but I desire, and I will not give God rest, but pray, till all my prayers be answered in heaven; and then I shall do the will of God as it is done in heaven indeed. Thus we ought eagerly, and constantly to persevere in our desires, till they be fully satisfied, or else we are but hypocrites.

Let us make conscience, I beseech you, of this duty more than we have done, and never give God

1 Matthew 6:10.

over for grace; for strength against our corruptions; for his church; for the prosperity of the means of salvation; for those things that we have ground for; let us never give him over till we see he has answered our desires. And when he has answered our desires, let us go on still to desire more; for this life is a life of desires. The life of accomplishment is heaven. Then all our desires shall be accomplished, and all promises performed, and not before then. This is a life of desires, and we must be in a state of desires and prayers still till we be in heaven.

QUESTION. What is the reason that God does not presently accomplish our desires?

ANSWER. There be diverse reasons. *First* of all *he loves to hear the desires of his servants*, he loves to be sued unto; because he knows it is for our good. It is music that best pleases God's ears to hear a soul come to him to request, especially spiritual things of him, which he delights most to give, which he knows is most useful and best for us. This pleases him so marvelously, that he will not presently grant it, but leads us along and along, that still he may hear more and more from us.

2. And then *to keep us in a perpetual humble subjection and dependence on him*, he grants not all at once, but leads us along, by yielding a little and a little, that so he may keep us in a humble dependence.

3. And then *to exercise all our graces;* for a

spirit of prayer is a spirit of exercise of all grace. We cannot pray, but we must exercise faith, and love to God and his church; and a sanctified judgment to esteem what are the best things to be prayed for; and to exercise mortification. "If I regard sin, God will not regard my prayers."[1] A spirit of prayer is a spirit that puts all into exercise; therefore God, to keep us in the exercise of all grace, answers not at the first.

4. And then he would have us *to set a high price upon what we desire and seek after.* If we had it at the first, we should not set so high an esteem and price of it.

5. And then, that *we might better use it when we have it.* Then we use things as we should do when we have gotten them with much ado; when we have won them from God with great importunity, then we keep and preserve them as we should. These and the like reasons may be given, and you may easily conceive them yourselves. Therefore let us not be offended with God's gracious dispensation if he answer not our desires presently, but pray still; and if we have the spirit of prayer continued to us, that spirit of prayer is better than the thing we beg a great deal. Ofttimes God answers us in a better kind, when he gives us a spirit of prayer; for increasing a spirit of prayer in us, he increases all graces in us. What is it we would have? this or that

1 Psalm 66:18.

particular grace. But when God gives us a spirit of prayer, he answers us better than in the thing we ask, for there is all grace. He will answer in one kind or other. But I will not be large in these points. You see then what was the affection of the holy prophet, to that one thing. "One thing have I desired." And he did not only desire it, but turned his desire into a prayer. He prayed to God; and he not only prayed once or twice, but he seeks it still, till God vouchsafed to grant it.

OBJECTION. Well, but that that he prayed for, he was assured of, and therefore what need he pray for it? He had a promise, "He shall prepare a table before mine enemies, my cup doth overflow."[1] But what is that to this? These be things of this life. Oh! but, says he, God will be good to me in the things of another life, and all the days of my life too. "Doubtless the loving kindness of the Lord shall follow me all the days of my life, and I shall dwell in the house of the Lord." He takes in trust his dwelling in the house of God; and that the loving kindness of God should follow him all the days of his life, he was assured of it, and yet here he seeks it and prays for it.

ANSWER. I note it, to show that the assurance of the thing takes not away the earnestness of prayer. Daniel was assured[2] that God would deliver the

1 Psalm 23:5, 6.
2 Daniel 4:4, seq.

Jews out of Babylon. He had read Jeremiah's prophecies, he knew the time was accomplished; yet we see what an earnest prayer he makes there. Christ knew that God heard him in all his desires, that he should have all good from God, being his only Son, yet he prayed whole nights sometimes, and a whole chapter, John 17, is an excellent prayer of his. So that the assurance of the thing takes not away prayer to God; nay, it establishes it, for God so makes good his promises for the time to come, as that he makes them good this way, he will be sought to by prayer. And I may know hence that he will make good his promises for the time to come to me, if I have a spirit of prayer for them; if I pray for perseverance to the end, that God would vouchsafe me grace to live in the church, and to grow up as a cedar. God surely means to grant this, because he has given me holy and gracious desires, which he would not have given me, but that he means to give the thing. For this is an encouragement to pray, when I know I shall not lose my labor. I pray, because I have a promise to have it, and I know the promise runs upon this. "But I will be sought unto of the house of Judah for this."[1] For if we have it, and have not sought it by prayer, for the most part we cannot have a comfortable use of it, unless we have things as the fruit of our prayers. Though there be not a particular prayer for every particular

1 Ezekiel 36:87.

thing we have of God, yet unless it be the fruit of the general prayer, that we put up daily, we cannot have comfort in it; if God give it by a general providence, as he fills "the bellies of the wicked with good things."[1] But if we will have things for our good in particular, we must receive them as the fruit of our prayers from God. You see here he seeks, and desires that that he had a promise to have, "One thing have I desired of the Lord, and that will I seek."

"That I may dwell in the house of the Lord."

It was generally propounded before. "One thing have I desired, and that will I seek after," with all my might. And what is that? The specification of it is this:

"That I may dwell in the house of the Lord for ever."

His desire is, not only to be in God's house, but to dwell in it, to abide; and not for a little while, but to dwell, and to dwell "all the days of my life."

The house of God then was the tabernacle, the sanctuary. The temple was not yet built. He desired to be near the tabernacle, to dwell in the sanctuary, the place of God's worship. In the tabernacle, which in those times was the house of God, there was the ark and the mercy-seat, types of many glorious things in the New Testament; the holy of holies, etc. And he desired to dwell in the tabernacle, to be near the ark, the house of God. Why?

1 Psalm 17:14.

Because God manifested his presence there, more than in other places. The ark has God's name in diverse places of Scripture; because God gave his answers in the ark, in the propitiatory, or mercy-seat. They came there to know his meaning, what he would have; he gave his answer there. He is said to dwell between the cherubim. There were two cherubim upon the mercy-seat, and God is said to dwell between the cherubim,[1] that is, there he was present to give answers to the high priest, when he came to ask. David knew this well enough, that God had vouchsafed a more special presence in the tabernacle, than in all the places of the world, and therefore, says he, "I desire to dwell in the house of the Lord all the days of my life."

"House," we take for the persons that are in it, and persons that are ordered, or else it is a confusion, and not a house. It is a company of those that are voluntary. They come not by chance into our house, those that are members of our society; but there is an order. There is a governor in a house, and some that are under government, and there is a voluntary conjunction and combination. So the church is a voluntary company of people that is orderly, some to teach, and some to be instructed; and thereupon it is called a house.

And it is called the house of God, because he is present there, as a man delights to be present in

1 Exodus 35:22.

his house. It is the place where God will be met
withal. As a man will be found in his house, and
there he will have suitors come to him, where he
reveals his secrets. A man rests, he lies, and lodges
in his house. Where is a man so familiar as in his
house? And what other place has he such care to
protect and provide for as his house? And he lays up
his treasures, and his jewels in his house. So God lays
up all the treasures of grace and comfort in the visible church. In the church he is to be spoken with as
a man is in his house. There he gives us sweet meet-
ings; there are mutual spiritual kisses. "Let him kiss
me with the kisses of his mouth."[1] A man's house
is his castle, as we say, that he will protect and provide for. God will be sure to protect and provide for
his church. Therefore he calls the church of God,
that is, the tabernacle (that was the church at that
time), the house of God. If we apply it to our times,
that that answers the tabernacle now, is particular
visible churches under particular pastors, where
the means of salvation are set up. Particular visible
churches now are God's tabernacle. (*b.*) The church
of the Jews was a national church. There was but
one church, but one place, and one tabernacle; but
now God has erected particular tabernacles. Every
particular church and congregation under one pas-
tor, their meeting is the church of God, a several
church independent. Our national church, that is,

1 Song of Solomon 1:2.

the Church of England, because it is under a government civil, which is not dependent upon any other foreign prince, it is a particular church from other nations.

In that God calls the church his house, it shows the special respect that he has to his church. God, though he be present everywhere, yet he is present in another manner in his church. As for instance, the soul is present in all the parts of the body; but the soul, as far as it understands, is only in the brain; as far as it is the fountain of life, it is in the heart. It has offices and functions in all the parts; but in the special function, the rational function of it, as it discourses and reasons, it is in the brain. So for our apprehension's sake, God is everywhere; but as he sanctifies and pours out his blessings, and opens, and manifests his secrets, so he is in his church especially. God is everywhere, but he is in another way in heaven than in other places. He is there gloriously. So in earth he is everywhere, but he is in another manner in the church (the heaven upon earth), than in other places. He is there as in his house to protect them, and provide for them as his family; and there he abides by his ordinances, and takes solace, and delight. God delights himself in his church and children that attend upon his ordinances. "Where two or three are met together, I will be in the midst of them."[1] When God's people

1 Matthew 18:20.

meet together in the church, God is present among them. So you see in what respect the tabernacle then, and particular churches now, which answer it, are called the house of God.

Let us learn this for our duty, as well as consider our comfort, in that the church is the house of God, *let us carry ourselves as we should, decently, in the house of God.* Those that are to look to the house of God, they should purge out all unclean corners, that God may delight to dwell in his house still, that we give him no cause to depart out of his house. "That I may *dwell in the house of the Lord.*" etc.

The act here is, that I "may dwell in house of the Lord." He did not desire to be in it for a day or a little time, to salute it, and so leave to it; but to "dwell in the house of the Lord," and to dwell there for ever. You see here that Christians have a constant love to the best things, a constant desire to dwell in the house of God. You may think it a strange desire of this holy man to dwell in the house of God; but think then of the continuedness of his desire, it was even to heaven itself; he desired "to dwell in the house of God for ever."

For what end?

1. I desire to dwell in the house of God, that I may dwell *in the love of God, and in the care of God to me in Christ for ever.* I do not desire to dwell in the house of God, as it is a meeting, and

there an end; but I desire to dwell in the house of
God, that I may dwell in the love and care of God,
and not only dwell in his care and love to me, and
his care and esteem of me; but,

2. That I may dwell *in my love to him*, that I
may "abide in his love," and faith in him; that I may
abide in Christ. It is not only for a man to abide in
the house of God, and go no further than so, but to
abide in the love of God; and in our love, and care,
and faith, and dependence upon him, to make God
our house, to live, and walk, and abide in, "to dwell
in God," as St. John says,[1] not only in the house of
God, but God himself. And the upshot of all his
desire, was to abide in heaven for ever. The desires of
God's people never rest till they come to their proper
center, and there they are quiet. There is a rest of all
desires in heaven; as fire, it never rests till it come to
its element above, and heavy bodies rest not till they
come to the center below. So holy desires, that are
the motion of the soul, they rest not till they come
to the center, the place of rest. So we must conceive
of David's desire to dwell in the house of the Lord,
to dwell in the care, and love, and protection of God
for ever, to dwell in love, and faith, and dependence,
and in the whole stream of my soul for ever while I
live; and then abide in heaven, where there are "pleasures for evermore," as he says in another place.[2]

1 1 John 4:13.
2 Psalm 16:11.

Therefore when we have any thoughts and desires, while we are here below, of grace and comfort, etc., let us extend, and stretch our desires to the last, to heaven itself, where all desires shall be accomplished, where all promises shall have their full performance. It is a poor thing only to desire to live in the church militant, and there is an end. No; here is the comfort of God's people, that in their prayers and desires, and their endeavors suitable to their prayers and desires, they all lead them to heaven; and there they have their full accomplishment. They have a constant desire to dwell in the house of God.

1. The reason is, because the soul in this world *is never fully satisfied with the good things of God's house till it be in heaven.* This life is a life of desires and longing; the church is but contracted to Christ in this world; the marriage shall be consummate in another world. Therefore the church desires still further and further communion with Christ in his ordinances here, and for ever in heaven.

2. And then *there are remainders of corruptions still, that dead and dull our performances, and put us on to actions that grieve our spirits and the Spirit of God;* to this end, that we may have a perpetual supply of the Spirit. We desire to dwell in the house of the Lord, because there is corruption in us still, till grace has wrought it out fully.

3. *There is more and more to be had still in the*

house of God. We never come to be full. The soul it is wondrous capable, being a spiritual essence. It is capable of more grace and comfort than we can have in this world. Therefore we pray, "Thy will be done on earth as it is in heaven." A Christian desires to dwell in the house of the Lord here, till he come to dwell in heaven, till he be translated from the temple here, to the temple in heaven. In Ephesians 4:11, seq., God has ordained a ministry to the edification of the church, not only to constitute the church, as some think and say, that preaching must constitute a church, and after praying must edify it. Oh! let both go together. "God gave gifts to men," to preach, to edify the church more and more. So long as there is use of building more and more, so long there is need of the ministry. Therefore he desired to "dwell in the house of the Lord."

4. But the especial reason why he desired it, was *because he knew God was also present in his own house, and there is no good thing can be wanting where God is present.* It is the presence of God that makes all things sweet and comfortable. What makes heaven to be heaven, but because God is there? If the soul of a Christian were among angels, angelical comforts would not be desired, if God were not there. If there were all the delights in the world, it would not care for them, except God were present. Heaven were not heaven without the presence of God. The presence of God in a dungeon, in

a lion's den, makes it a paradise, a place of pleasure; the presence of God makes all conditions comfortable. If there be not the presence of God, the greatest comfort in the world is nothing. What makes the church esteemed of by holy men? God is present there; and wheresoever God is present, in the communion of saints, especially in his ordinances, we should esteem them by this, that God is present. What makes hell to be hell? There is no presence of God there; no testimony of his presence in hell; nothing but "utter darkness." What makes the life of man comfortable? There is some presence of God in everything. There is a presence of God in meat, in drink, in friends, that a man may say, Oh, here is a good God, here is some presence of God. There is not the vilest reprobate in the world, but he has some testimony of God's presence. He tastes of God in somewhat or other; though he see not God in it (but like a beast is drowned in the use of the creature), yet God shows himself to him in some comfort. But when God shall remove all his presence from a man, that is hell itself. What is hell but where there is no presence of God? When there is no communion with the chief good, that the fountain of good is removed, a man is in darkness, and horror, that is hell, as we see in Dives.[1] It is the presence of God that makes things comfortable. That is heaven, to enjoy nearer and nearer communion with God.

1 Luke 16:4, seq.

Therefore let us labor to enjoy the presence of God in his ordinances, that we may have a heaven upon earth, that we may desire still more and more to delight in them, till we come to heaven, where all desires shall be accomplished, and there shall be no more desire. David knowing that God was present in his church, he says, "Oh that I might dwell in the house of God all the days of my life."

See the constant disposition of God's children hence. It is a torment to carnal men to watch one hour with Christ. "Could you not watch with me one hour?"[1] says he to his disciples. It is a torment to give God the hearing; to sanctify the Lord's Day. Alas! it cannot stand with their carnal dispositions. But God's people long, and have a longing desire. "One thing have I desired, that I may dwell in the house of the Lord." Men that have not depth of grace, they are like comets. They blaze for a time; but when they are not fed with vapors from below, there is a disparition not long after. But fixed stars are always in the firmament; they never vary. So a true Christian is as a fixed star, he is fixed in the firmament, in his desire. "One thing have I desired, that I may dwell in the house of the Lord all the days of my life;" and God seconds his desire, and says amen to it; as I shall have occasion to press after, in the use in the latter part of the verse. "That I may dwell in the house of the Lord."

1 Matthew 26:40.

"To behold the beauty of the Lord."

This was another ground of the eager, constant, unsatisfied desire, "To dwell in the house of the Lord," that he might "see the beauty of the Lord," or the delight, the sweetness of God. Beauty is too particular a word to express the fullness of the Holy Ghost, the pleasantness or the delight of God. Take the word in a general sense, in your apprehensions. It may be the object of all senses, inward and outward. Delight is most transcendent for pleasantness; for indeed God in his ordinances, is not only beauty to the eye of the soul, but is ointment to the smell, and sweetness to the taste, and all in all to all the powers of the soul. God in Christ, therefore, he is delightful and sweet. "That I may see the beauty of the Lord."

In this clause here are discovered these two things, the object and the act.

There are these two points. *That God is beautiful.* And this is seen in his ordinances, and in his church, especially, "to see the beauty" of God's house. And *it is the happiness of a Christian*, and he esteems it so by the Spirit of God, to see, and to be partaker of this beauty of God. Sight is put for the more full enjoying, one sense put for another, as indeed sight is taken for all the senses, inward and outward. It is no benefit to us, though there be beauty, if we have not eyes to see it, all is lost; therefore he desired to dwell in the house of the Lord, that he might "see the beauty of the Lord."

Now, concerning the beauty of God, I will not speak of it at large, or singly of the excellencies of God. The text aims especially at the beauty of God, *as discovered in his ordinances, in his church*. A man may speak gloriously, and largely of the beauty of God, of his excellency. That his wisdom is wondrous excellent, and beautiful, that is seen in the ordering of things, and his power is wonderful beautiful, and his mercy, etc. All this is true; but what is all to us, though God be never so beautiful in himself, if he be not beautiful to us in Christ, and in his church? Therefore we will come to that that the holy prophet here aims at, "The beauty of the Lord;" that is, God is especially beautiful in his church, in his ordinances, and that was the ground of his desire. *Omne pulchrum est amabile*, every beautiful thing is an attractive of love. It is no wonder he desired to dwell in the house of the Lord, because there was the beauty of the Lord, and the most excellent beauty of all.

The beauty of the Lord is especially the amiable things of God, which is his mercy and love, that makes all other things beautiful that is in the church.

What makes his power sweet to his children? and his justice, in confounding their enemies, and giving rewards? and his wisdom sweet, in reconciling justice and mercy together wisely in Christ? All that makes this so lovely, is his grace and love, that set his wisdom on work, to devise a way to reconcile justice and mercy by Christ Emmanuel, God and man. So that that is most beautiful in God is grace; as you have it.[1] When Moses desired to see the glory of God, how does God describe himself to Moses? "Jehovah, Jehovah strong, gracious, merciful, long-suffering, full of kindness." So that if we would see the glory of God, it appears most in grace, and mercy, and loving-kindness, and such sweet attributes. This makes all things in God amiable; for now we can think of his justice, and not fear. It is fully satisfied in Christ. We can think of his power with comfort. It serves for our good to subdue all our enemies. There is no attribute, though it be terrible in itself, but it is sweet and amiable, because God looks graciously on us in his beloved.

Now this grace and love and mercy of God shines to us in the face of Christ as beloved, as I have showed out of that text, 2 Corinthians 3:18, We all behold the glory of God as in a glass (c.), that is, we behold the love of God in Jesus Christ, in the mirror of the gospel. We must take God, not as considered abstractively[2] and simply, but God in Christ; for other notions of God are terrible. God will not otherwise be seen by the eye of the soul, nor otherwise known, than in Christ. Now God

1 Exodus 34:6.
2 That is, "abstractly."—G.

in the Messiah is very delightful in his house. This beauteous grace of God shines in the face of Jesus Christ.[1] For God is so gracious and merciful, as that his justice must be fully satisfied, that is, only in Christ; that being satisfied, God in Christ looks on us with a gracious look. So that God is beautiful now in regard of his mercy and grace, as it is revealed in Jesus Christ, as he looks upon us in the face of his beloved Son. There are two objects of religious worship. God the Father, Son, and Holy Ghost, and Christ Mediator. The beauty of both is wondrous in the church, wondrous towards the church of God, and it is most apparent in the ordinances of God in the church. Christ is "altogether lovely."[2] Christ in whom God is a Father, and reconciled to us; and now we can sweetly think of, "He is altogether lovely, the chief of ten thousand." The church sets him out there particularly, his head, his arms, his breasts, his eyes. "His lips drop myrrh."[3] She singles out every excellency of Christ, and dwells upon it in her meditation, and sums up all together, "Christ is lovely." What makes beauty but a mixture of diverse colors? as we say, white and red mix together sweetly. Now to see justice and mercy in Christ so sweetly mixed, what an excellent beauty it makes! To see the justice of God fully

---

1 2 Corinthians 4:6.
2 Song of Solomon 5:16.
3 Song of Solomon 5:13.

satisfied, that his mercy might run amain to us now. Here is a sea indeed if we should enter into it, to see the love of God, which is the most beautiful and amiable grace of all; the love of God in Christ, and the love of Christ towards us.

Christ was never more lovely to his church than when he was most deformed for his church; "there was no form nor beauty in him,"[1] when he hung upon the cross. Oh! there was a beauty to a guilty soul, to see his surety enduring the wrath of God, overcoming all his enemies, and nailing the law to his cross. And that should endear Christ to us above all things. He should be the dearer to us, the more vile and base he was made for us, and he should be most lovely in our eyes, when he was least lovely in his own, and when he was deformed, when our sins were upon him. We should consider those times especially. The world is most offended at that, that a Christian most joys in. "God forbid that I should joy in anything but in the cross of Christ,"[2] says St. Paul; so we should joy in and love that especially in Christ.

Now this love of God in Christ, and this love of Christ, is expressed to us in the Scriptures at large; it is published by the ministry, sealed by the sacrament. It is too large an argument for me to wade into. I need but only give you a touch and taste of it.

1 Isaiah 53:2.
2 Galatians 6:14.

Now, that that makes the house of God so beautiful, then, *is the love of God, and the love of Christ showed and manifested, and the presence of God, of Christ, and of the Holy Ghost in the church.* Take it for the persons; God the Father, as he has revealed himself a Father in Christ, he is among the people of God in the church, and there is God the Son, and the Holy Ghost, dispensing graces and comfort there. It is the presence of the king that makes the court, and it is the presence of God in the church that makes it so glorious and so excellent as it is. "Glorious things are spoken of thee, thou city of God."[1]

The church likewise is beautiful *in regard of the angels, that are always attending in our assemblies,* and see how we carry ourselves. Here is not only the Father, Son, and Holy Ghost distributing grace and mercy, but likewise the blessed angels, as pure instruments are in our assemblies. Therefore in the curtains, in the hangings of the ark, there were pictures of cherubim, to show that the angels attend about the church, especially the church gathered together; for God more respects the church gathered together than any several member. We are all temples severally, but especially the church is the temple when it is met together. Now by the cherubim in the curtains of the tabernacle, was set forth the angels' attendance upon the church. They are

1 Psalm 87:3.

servants to do good to the church; and they are fellow-students with us. They study the mysteries of salvation, the beauty of God, the wonderful transcendent love, and grace, and mercy of God to his church, as it is in 1 Peter 1:10, 11. "The angels pry into the mysteries of salvation;" they are students with us of those blessed mysteries. Something is revealed to them, some grace and mercy to the church, that they knew not before experimentally.

And it is beautiful likewise in regard *of the church itself.* The people of God themselves are beautiful; for order is beautiful. Now it is an orderly thing to see many together to submit themselves to the ordinance of God. "The glory of a king is in the multitude of subjects,"[1] and it is a glorious thing for God to have many subjects meekly meeting together to attend his pleasure. An army is a beautiful thing, because of the order, and of the well disposed ranks that are within it. In this regard the church is beautiful.

That which makes the house of God beautiful more especially, *is the means of salvation:* not only God's presence, but the means, solemn and public prayer, the word and sacraments, and likewise the government, that should be in purging the church—all make the church of God beautiful and lovely. All the ordinances of God in the church of God have a delight in them to spiritual senses.

1   Proverbs 14:28.

1. *As for the ordinance of the Word*, it is wondrous delightful, "sweeter than the honeycomb,"[1] especially the ordinance unfolding the Word, the Word as it is preached, which is the "opening of the box." A box of sweet ointment, if it be not opened, it casts not a sweet savor all the house over; but when the box is opened, the savor comes over all the house. So the publishing of the Word in the ordinance, is the opening of the box, the lifting up of the brazen serpent. If the serpent were [not] lift up for the wounded person, he could not behold it. Now [that] Christ is lift up in the ordinance, every wounded soul may look to Christ. The preaching of the Word, is the lifting up of the banner of Christ's love. As it is in the Canticles, Christ's love as a banner draws all after him. When the beauty of Christ is unfolded, it draws the wounded, hungry soul unto him. The preaching of the Word does that that shows the sweet love of God in Jesus Christ. This makes the ordinance of the ministry so sweet. The ordinance of the ministry is that that distributes the portion to every child of God. The ministers of God are stewards, as it were, to distribute comfort and reproof to whom it belongs. Now where there is a convenient distributing of the portion to every one, that makes the ordinance of God so beautiful, when the waters of life are derived from the spring of the Scripture to every particular man's use. The Word,

1 Psalm 19:10.

in the application of it, is a sweet thing. For good things, the nearer they are brought home, the more delightful they are. This ordinance of preaching, it lays open the "riches of Christ." There may be a great deal of riches wrapped up in a treasury, but this opens the treasury, as St. Paul says, "to lay open the unsearchable riches of Christ."[1] The ministry of the Word is ordained to lay open the treasure to God's people, that they may know what riches they have by Christ; and the end of the ministry is to win the people's love to Christ. Therefore they come between the bride and bridegroom to procure the marriage; therefore they lay open that that procures the contract here, and the consummation in heaven; so to woo for Christ, and "beseech them to be reconciled to God."[2] This is the end of the ministry. This makes the church of God so beautiful, that it has this ordinance in it, to bring God, and Christ, and his people together: to contract them together. There be rich mines in the Scripture, but they must be dug up. The ministry serves to dig up those mines. God has therefore set apart this calling of the ministry, to show what belongs to God's people. Thus you see in this respect, of the ordinance of the ministry, God is beautiful in his house.

2. Then likewise for the other ordinance, *the sacrament, it is a sweet and delightful thing*. There is a

1 Ephesians 3:8.
2 2 Corinthians 5:20.

wondrous beauty in the sacrament; for therein we taste the love of God, and the love of Christ. That they would condescend so low, as to seal our faith with the sacrament, to help our souls by our bodies, by outward things; to help our souls by that that feeds our bodies, to teach us what feeds our souls, namely, the death of Christ, as satisfying divine justice—the thinking and digesting of this is wondrous comfortable, as any food is to the body, and incomparably more sweet, considering our continual necessity to relish that spiritual food, and our daily sins and breaches, that enforce a daily necessity to relish Christ. That God should appoint such means, that he should in the sacrament feed us with his own body and blood. He thought he could not manifest his love enough, unless he had told us that he would give himself to us, and make over himself wholly to us: You shall have me; my body and blood; as in the sacrament we are as verily partakers of the body and blood of Christ, as we are of the bread and wine. Our souls have as much spiritual growth by Christ, and his benefits, as our bodies have by the outward elements. He feeds us with himself; he esteems and prizes our souls that are bought with his blood, so that he thinks no food good enough but his own body and blood. What a gracious sweet love is this! He is both the inviter and the banquet, and all. He invites us to himself.

3. There is a loveliness likewise *in all other*

ordinances that belong to the church; as in the good order and government of the church, in purging the church of offenders; the discipline that is in the church, which is as the snuffers in the sanctuary to purge the lights; so that there should be a casting out of persons that are openly scandalous. The lights should be purged, the temple should be cleansed, scandals should be removed, that God's house might be the more beautiful. They are blemishes of God's house, open swearers and blasphemers. Those that live in scandalous sins, they are spots in the assembly, they are leaven, and this leaven should be purged out; and where there is the vigor of this, there is a great beauty of the church. Where these things are looked to as they should be, they are the bonds, and nerves, and sinews that knit and tie a church together. It makes a church wondrous lovely, the neglect of which makes the church as a garden overgrown. So you see how, in respect of the ordinances of the Word, and of the sacrament, and this government that should be, that the house of God is a beautiful place.

4. Then again, it is a comfortable, a sweet and delightful thing, *the praises of God.* It is a marvellous sweet thing, when all as one man hear together, pray together, sing together hymns, and spiritual songs, and praise God together, and receive the sacrament together, all as one man—what a comely thing is this to a spiritual eye! Every Christian has

a beauty severed in himself; but when all meet together, this is more excellent. As we say of the *via lactea*, or milky way in the heavens (we call it so), it is nothing but a deal of light from a company of little stars, that makes a glorious luster. So if there be a beauty in every poor Christian, what a beauty is there when all meet together! A beauty, nay, strength too; for the prayer and the praise of such, they offer a holy violence to God, they can obtain anything at his hands. We see burning glasses, when there is a confluence, and meeting of divers beams in one point, it strengthens the heat, and inflames a thing; so when there are many sweet desires meet together, many strong desires of spiritual things, they bind God. There is not only beauty but strength in the prayers of the church. They are in Christ's own esteem comeliness. He loves to see his church, especially when they are together. "Let me see thy face, and hear thy voice, thou that hidest thyself in the clefts of the rock."[1] He marvelously desires to see his children, and to hear them speak, especially when they present themselves before him. Harmony is a sweet and pleasant thing. The comparing of the state of the church in former times with the present, is a harmonious thing. David, he lived under the Old Testament, and yet he saw under that the New, so we should see the Old in the New, compare them together, to see shadows in substances, types

1 Song of Solomon 2:14.

in truths. So that there is nothing in the church, but it gives special delight.

5. God's beauty likewise appears, his gracious, amiable, sweet beauty, in his house, his church in regard *of the evidences of his love that he bears to his church, in protecting it, and providing for it.* "They shall not need a wall," says he in Zechariah, "I will be a wall of fire."[1] God has a special care of his congregation. "God dwells in the congregation of the righteous."[2] He has his dwelling, his special residence there, where his name is called on. This will appear more if we see all the sweet privileges and comforts that are in the house of God. God is not only beautiful in himself, but in regard of the privileges that the church has from him. For all our beauty and excellency is borrowed. The church shines in the beams and beauty of Christ. Now these privileges that the church has by Christ, to name a few. (1.) *We see in the golden chain of salvation,* what sweet, amiable love is in all those links; as what a wondrous sweet love of God is it. (2.) *To call men out of the wilderness of the world,* out of the kingdom of Satan, to be his children! A marvellous love to single us out of the rest of mankind to be Christians, and being Christians, to be professors of the truth, and being so, to be true professors of the truth. What a wondrous love of God was it to call

---

1 Zechariah 2:5.
2 Psalm 82:1.

us, and thereby to have the eternal purpose of God opened to us. As when we are drawn to God by his Spirit and by the ministry, then the good pleasure of God, that was hid from eternity, is discovered to the soul. Here is the amiable love of God.

(3.) And then in *the pardon, and forgiveness of sins, and justification after*—what a wondrous grace is that forgiveness of sins, and adoption to be the sons and heirs of God, "fellow-heirs with Jesus Christ,"[1] and thereupon to have angels our attendants. What beauty have we in justification, to be clothed with the righteousness of Christ; that perfect righteousness, that can answer the justice of God much more Satan's cavils and the troubles of our own consciences. That that satisfies the justice of God, being the righteousness of God-man, it will satisfy conscience, and Satan's temptations. It is a garment without spot. Satan can pick no hole in that glorious garment, the righteousness of Christ. If we have the wardrobe of Christ, we shall be beautiful in that we have from Christ, we shall shine in his beams.

(4.) So go to *sanctification*. How amiable is God in the privilege of sanctification, to set his image upon us, to make us new creatures, to be like his Son, that before were like the devils, full of malice and base affections. Now for God by his Spirit to frame a new temple for his Spirit to dwell in, to

1 Romans 8:17.

set his stamp upon us, what a wondrous beauty is this! The church of God is the house where God frames new creatures. There he sets a stamp upon his creatures.

The graces that belong to the church of God are wondrous delight. "Wisdom makes a man's face to shine,"[1] and there is no wisdom out of the church. All is but darkness and folly. So of all other graces whatsoever. Graces are the anointing of the Spirit, the oil of the Spirit. They make sweet and delightful, delightful to God, and to the church, and to one another. They are anointed with the oil of gladness and of grace. It ran first upon Christ's head, upon Aaron's head, but then upon the skirts, the meanest Christian.

And so the beginning of glory here; for all is not kept for the life to come. For God distils some drops of glory beforehand. We see the beauty of God here, marvelously even in this world, in regard of the beginning of glory. For upon justification, and the beginning of holiness wrought in our nature by the Spirit, we have inward peace of conscience, and joy and comfort in all discomforts whatsoever. We have not only the oil of grace, but the oil of comfort. Oh! the comfort of the children of God, that are members of the church, that are so in the church, that they are of the church too, that are of the church visible, so as they are of the

1 Ecclesiastes 8:1.

church invisible. Oh! the comfort that belongs to them, all the comfort in God's book. So you see the wondrous sweet prerogatives and privileges we have in all the passages of salvation in the house of God, and in God reconciled in Jesus Christ.

Nay, God is so lovely to those that are his, his church and people, he is so good to Israel, that he makes everything good to them in the issue. "All things work for the best to them that love God,"[1] in the issue. He makes a covenant between everything. So that all the endeavors of Satan and his instruments, all their plottings, shall turn for the good of the church. When they think to do most hurt, they do most good; so sweet, and good, and gracious is God.

Indeed, "glorious things are spoken,"[2] of the people of God. Take the church for a visible congregation, a mixed congregation; glorious things are spoken of that. It is the house of God. Take it as visible, "the vessels of honor and dishonor,"[3] and the field, the "tares and the wheat,"[4] it is God's field. Though we take the church as visible, it has a glorious name for the good that is in it, specially for the wheat. But take the church of God for the company of his children that are gathered by the means dwelling in the visible church, enjoying the visible means: so they

---

1 Romans 8:28.
2 Psalm 87:3.
3 2 Timothy 2:20.
4 Matthew 13:1, seq.

are the house and temple of Christ, the "temple of the Holy Ghost, the body of Christ, the spouse of Christ." They are God's delight, they are spiritual kings and priests, etc. The most glorious things that can be, all other excellencies in the world, are but titular things, mere shadows of things. There is some little reality, but it is nothing in comparison, it is scarce worth the name of reality, but Solomon calls them "vanity of vanities." In comparison of the excellencies of the church all is nothing. I might be large in these particulars. It is enough to give you the generals of the delights and excellencies of God's house, "the beauty of the Lord." We see amiableness of God in Christ, in his ordinances, the privileges that we have in the ordinances, graces, and comforts. Indeed the church of God, beloved, is a paradise. Since we were cast out of the first paradise, this second paradise is the church of God, and the third is heaven itself. This paradise, this church, it is the seminary[1] of young plants, that must be transplanted hence to heaven in due time. In paradise there was the tree of life,[2] in the church, there is the tree of life, Christ. In paradise there was waters, streams, the rivers of paradise,[3] so there "is a river that makes glad the city of God,"[4] streams of grace

---

1 That is, "seed-plot."—G.

2 Genesis 3:22.

3 Genesis 2:10.

4 Psalm 46:4.

and comfort that run through the church of God.

In the church we are as plants by the rivers of waters, that bring forth fruit in due season, as it is in Psalm 1:3, seq. Speaking of blessed men that live in the church, "Blessed is the man that meditates in the word day and night," that attends upon the ordinances. He is "planted as a tree by the waters' side," his leaf is always green. What food to that food that is ministered to us in the Word, and sacraments—Christ himself to feed us to life eternal! And what raiment to the raiment of justification; for Christ to clothe these poor souls of ours, poor, naked, beggarly souls! What riches to the riches of God's graces and comforts! What strength to that that is in the church, to overcome our own corruptions and lusts! What beauty to the image of God shining and stamped on his children! What company so sweet, as those that we meet with in the earth, in good exercises, and that we shall live ever with in heaven! What company to God the Father, Son, and Holy Ghost, and the angels, that we enjoy in the church! What discourse so sweet, as that of God, hearing him speak in his word, and us speaking to him by prayer, so that it is a resemblance of heaven upon earth, the church of God!

Therefore we should be in love with the beauty of God's temple and sanctuary. And the rather because all things now in this age of the church wherein we live are in a more glorious manner than in David's time. David when he saw the beauty of God's sanctuary, it was but in a shadow; and when he looked upon the mercy-seat, then he did think of Christ, the true propitiatory, the true mercy-seat. When he looked on the high priest, he thought on Christ the true high priest. When he thought of Canaan, it put him in mind of heaven, whereof Canaan was a type. When he saw the sacrifices, he thought of the true sacrifice for our sins, Christ. When he thought of the oblations and incense, he thought of the sacrifice of thankfulness. When he thought of the Passover, he thought of Christ the true Passover, whose blood is sprinkled on our souls, that the destroying angel has nothing to do with us. He saw all in shadows; we see them naked. So our condition is more glorious in this latter age of the church, than it was in David's time. Therefore our desires should be more stirred up; for instead of the shadow we have the substance. Then the Spirit was but dropped, but the Father has poured out the Spirit since Christ's time. Then the pale of the church was straitened, now it is enlarged. Then there was but one church, the national church of the Jews. Then the service of God was wondrous burdensome, and chargeable, but it is not so now. So that there be many differences. All things are more lightsome and clear now than they were then. Therefore having many things to commend the frequenting of the congregation more than David had in his time, we should much more make this one thing our desire "to dwell in the house of the Lord, all the days of our life, to *behold the beauty of the Lord.*"

QUESTION 1. If this be so, that there is such a beauty in the house of God, then what shall we think of those that see no such beauty at all, that see no such delight and contentment in the house of God?

ANSWER 1. I answer, it is a discovery to them, if they would think of it, *that they have no spiritual senses at all;* as St. Austin says of men that complain, that they do not taste and relish these things. Surely, says he, you want a spiritual palate to taste these things. What do swine care for sweet marjoram or roses? They care more for a dunghill or a puddle. What do your base filthy swine in men's shape care for these things? They care more for pleasures and such things, that they may spend their lives as beasts. Now when we speak of the delights, and dainties, and excellencies of God's house, we speak to those that we wish, and we hope have spiritual senses answerable to these things. Every creature delights in its proper element. These things are the element of a Christian. Beetles delight in dirt, and swine in mire, the fish in the sea, man has his element here, and spiritual things are the element of a Christian, so far as he is a Christian, and that is his *ubi*, the place that he delights in. I speak to such. They can make it good in some measure, that "one day in the house of God is better than a thousand elsewhere,"[1] that one hour in the unfolding the sweet mysteries of salvation, it is worth twenty-four hours in other employment; and they are so taken with the sweetness, that they are content that God should take them out of the world, in the unfolding of these sweet things. When they hear the promises of salvation opened, though by a poor weak man, yet when it is in the ministry, it so ravishes their hearts, that they are content to go to heaven at the same time; it so convinces them of the excellency of religion. I speak to such of the beauty of God.

Now David here, he desires to behold God's beauty, to see or consider this excellency of God in his church, for to true delight these things must concur. There must be something sweet in the thing itself. There must be a power in the soul to apprehend it. There must be an affection in the soul to that good thing. If the affection be flat, though there be never so beautiful and sweet things, and a power to apprehend them, if there be not affection, they are nothing; and then, upon the affection, there must be complacency and contentment in the thing when we have it. All these things are in delight from that that is beautiful and pleasant, David desired to see. He knew there was a beauty in the presence of God in his ordinances and gifts

1 Psalm 84:10.

and graces; but he desired to see and to contemplate these things, that the faculties and powers of his soul might be answerable to the things, that as they were excellent, so he might have a power in his soul answerable. And then he had affections to carry that power of his soul to the things, "One thing have I desired." And then there was a complacency and delight in the things, upon enjoining,[1] answerable, as we see how he expressed his delight when he danced before the ark. We see what a psalm he made when he did but purpose "to build the temple."[2] He had a wondrous joy. So answerable to our delights is our joy and complacency in the thing when we have it.

Now that he might have the sweeter complacency, he desired to see the beauty and the things in God's house. Of all senses, sight has this property above the rest (as it is more spiritual, more refined, and more capable; a man may see many things at once, it is a quick sense; so), it has this privilege, it stirs affections more than any sense, more than hearing, that is a more dull sense. Things stir affections more that are seen, than by that we hear. He desired therefore to see the beauty of God's house, that he might be enamoured. Of sight comes love.

David had spiritual eyes, and he desired to feed his spiritual eyesight with the best object

1 Qu. "enjoying?"—ED.
2 Psalm 132.

that could be, for therein is the happiness of man. Wherein stands a man's happiness? When there is a concurrence of the most excellent object, with the most excellent power and faculty of the soul, with delight and content in it. Now he desired to see the beauty of God in his house, that his soul might be ravished in the excellency of the object, and that the highest powers of his soul, his understanding, will, and affections might be fully satisfied, that he might have full contentment. Since the fall, all our happiness is out of ourselves, it is derived from God in Christ; and it is taken out of the promises of God in the Word. For God will be seen in Christ, and God and Christ will be seen in the glass of the ordinances till we come to heaven, and there we shall see "face to face."[1] So that now all our happiness is fetched by looking on the love of God, out of ourselves, fetched out of the ordinances. David desired to see the beauty of God. God's love is diffusive. It spreads and communicates itself to his church in the ordinances. Thus he, knowing, desired more and more to communicate of this diffusive, abundant, transcendent love of God.

QUESTION 2. But how shall we come to have these desires that David had, to see the beauty of God?

ANSWER 2. In a word—we must have *spiritual senses*. The spiritual life of a Christian is furnished

1 1 Corinthians 13:12.

with spiritual senses. He has a spiritual eye and a spiritual taste to relish spiritual things, and a spiritual ear to judge of holy things, and a spiritual feeling. As every life, so this excellent life has senses and motion suitable to it. Now we should labor to have this spiritual life quickened in us, that we may have a quick sight of heavenly things; and a taste of heavenly things, that we may smell the ointment of Christ. "For the sweetness of thy ointments the virgins run after thee."[1] The soul has senses answerable to the body, let us desire God *to cleanse all our senses, and to reveal himself in Christ more and more in the ordinances.*

This St. Paul calls the "Spirit of revelation."[2] Let us pray to God that in his ordinances he would discover that amiable love of his in Christ, to shine on us in the face of his Son, in his ordinances; for the Spirit must help us to see the beauty of God. When we have spiritual senses, except the Spirit give us a spiritual light to see, we cannot see. Therefore let us desire that God would give us spiritual senses, to the spiritual light.

When God made the world, light was the first creature. Why? That all the excellency of the creature might be discerned by light. If God had made never so many excellent creatures, if the light had not discovered them, where had been his glory?

1 Song of Solomon 1:3.
2 Ephesians 1:17.

So there are many excellent, beautiful things in Christ, wonderful grace and comfort; if these be discovered in the Word and we have no senses, and no light, if there be not light in the understanding, God shall want his glory, and we the comfort.

It is light that makes things that are beautiful to be beautiful to us. A blind man cannot judge of colors, nor a deaf man of sounds and harmony. A man that has lost his taste cannot judge of sweetness, so that there must be senses, and the Spirit of God must reveal these things unto us.

And likewise let us labor more and more to *see our own deformity, and then we shall see Christ's beauty, the more we desire to know our own vileness.* Indeed the Spirit of God carries these parallel one with another. He discovers by the same light our own deformity and necessity, and the beauty and excellency of God in Jesus Christ. The one will set an edge on the other, and he that will come to see the height and breadth, and depth of God's love in Christ, must see the height, and breadth, and depth of his own corruption, and our misery by it out of Christ. And they are good thoughts for us, every day to think of these two objects, the misery of the condition of man out of Christ, and the excellency now that we have in Jesus Christ; the amiableness of Christ towards us, and our amiable condition in him. He delights in us, as we delight in him. The consideration of this, and of the loathsome, terrible, fearful condition out of him, will keep us closer to Christ, and make us value the ordinances more, that we may grow up in faith and knowledge of Christ more and more, till we come to a fullness in Christ.

And present to the eye of our souls, God in Christ *in the relations he has taken upon him*, to be a Father in Christ. Let us make that benefit of this beauty that is presented to us in the gospel, especially when it is unfolded in the ministry, because Satan has a special policy to present God and Christ otherwise to us. Especially in the time of temptation, he presents God as a judge, sitting upon his throne, and God as a "consuming fire."[1] It is true he is so out of Christ, but in him he has taken the relation of a father, and looks on us sweetly in the relation of sons. Christ must be considered in the sweet relation of a Saviour, and the Holy Ghost in the sweet relation of a comforter; and the Word is all written for our comfort, if we believe, and the sacraments feed us to eternal life. Let us represent these things beautifully to the soul, and this will strengthen faith, and cherish affection, that Satan shall not rob us of our comfort, nor say to us, what do you, ye unclean persons, loathsome creatures, what do you come to the sacrament, and come to the holy things of God? It is true, if we mean to be so still, but as soon as ever the desire of our souls is

1 Hebrews 12:29.

to come to God, and that there is a divorce between us and our sins, and we desire to leave them, let us have all the sweet conceits of God that may be. We see in Revelations, Laodicea was lukewarm, and that is a hateful temper. "Behold," says he, "I stand and knock, if any man open to me, I will come, and sup with them."[1] A strange love, to come to them that were in such a lukewarm estate. He was ready to cast them out. His stomach was loaden with them. "I stand at the door and knock," yet if any of you luke-warm professors will open, I will come and sup with him, and refresh him with the refreshings of God. So in Song of Solomon 5, when the church slighted Christ and offended him, yet he woos his church. My locks are wet with the dew of the night.[2] Oh! marvellous patience, that notwithstanding her luke-warmness and neglect, yet Christ gives not over! Let us not entertain hard conceits of God in Christ, but labor to present them sweetly to our meditations.

This is the wisdom of a Christian, to have sights of faith, that is, to present several things that faith may work on to strengthen itself, as for faith to have a sight of God in Christ, a gracious Father; and to have a spiritual sight of Christ sending ambassadors wooing and beseeching us to be reconciled; and a sight of the joys of heaven, that we shall have full possession of after. Let us think of them, and present

1 Revelation 3:20.
2 Song of Solomon 5:2.

them to our souls; and present to our souls by meditation, the excellency, and royalty, and prerogative of God's children, that they are the most excellent people in the world. These sights that faith helps itself by, are an excellent means to make us in love with the beauty of God's house. But to answer two or three objections briefly before I proceed to more particulars.

OBJECTION 1. Some will object, what need we now in these glorious times of the church stand upon the ordinances so much? Indeed in darker times there was more need, etc.

ANSWER 1. I will not be large, but to answer in a word. *The more God discovers himself, and his excellent things here, the more we should express our thankfulness in laboring to grow in knowledge;* for there is such a breadth in them, that we can never have enough of them, and there is such a daily exigence of spiritual things, of comforts and graces, that are all conveyed in the use of means, that a Christian cannot be without them; he can no more be without the use of the ordinances than he can without his daily food.

OBJECTION 2. Oh! but what need we be so eager and earnest after these things as some are? Is not now and then enough?

ANSWER 2. Are we better than David? See how earnest he was.[1] "As the hart panteth after the rivers

1 Psalm 84 and Psalm 42.

of water, so my soul thirsteth after thee, O God."[1] For there is a presence of God in his ordinances that other men are not sensible of. There is a presence to their spirits that they feel that they marvelously love, and are affected with. And if they want the presence of God, as David here, they are wondrously discouraged. As good Nehemiah, when he heard it went not well with the church, he grew sad; and David, we see how he takes it here when he was banished, as it were, from the house and ordinances of God. But I will not stand long upon these objections.

OBJECTION 3. Some think they may as well read at home good books and sermons, and not come to the ordinances.

ANSWER 3. But David *loved the ordinances; he loved the place.* Might not he think of what he heard before? might not he have help of the prophets? Oh! but there is a blessing in the very meeting, "Where two or three are met together, I will be in the midst of them."[2] And Christ walks in the midst "of the golden candlesticks."[3] There is a more powerful, gracious presence in the very assemblies of God's people. Put case[4] you may do much good in private, with contempt of the public ordinance; it is a

1 Psalm 42:1, 74:2.
2 Matthew 18:20.
3 Revelation 1:12.
4 Put case—suppose the case to be.

cursed study. Like manna that did stink when it was gathered out of season. When it was gathered when it should not, it putrefied. There is a curse upon that study, and upon that knowledge that we get when we should attend upon the public means. For it is not knowledge that will bring to heaven, for the devil has that, but it is knowledge sanctified, seizing upon the affections. Now, what is it that makes us good? The Spirit working with the ordinance; and will the Spirit work when we neglect the ordinance? It is but a pretence. They spend their time otherwise, it is to be feared not so well. But put the case they should, there never comes good of it. It may enrich them in knowledge to grow more devilish; but more holy they cannot be, for holiness comes from the Spirit, and the Spirit will work by his own ordinances. So much for that, and of all other objections in regard of the beauty of God.

I will not raise any objections, but only answer those that commonly popish spirits trouble some withal. I will answer, I say, some of them briefly.

OBJECTION 4. They trouble us about our churches. Indeed, if your particular churches were churches of God, if you could make that good, then you might delight in them, but you are heretics and schismatics; your churches are not good churches. Thus they trouble good Christians that are of the simpler sort; especially with this, where was your church a hundred years ago? before Luther's time? (*d.*) Your church is an upstart, and your congregations are nothing but a meeting of a company of heretics together.[1]

ANSWER 4. Beloved, that *that makes a church to be a catholic church, to be a branch of the catholic church*, which we believe in the creed, *it is the catholic faith*. The faith and truth that is the seed of the church, it is begotten of the Word of God. Wheresoever the Word, the catholic truth of God, is, there is the church, a branch of the catholic church. Now our faith that we believe has consanguinity with the first churches; for what do we believe, but it is fetched out of the Testament, and from the primitive church? And indeed in their own confession, if they would be modest, that might be extorted from them, that we are more catholic, and our doctrine is more catholic than theirs. Why? For that that agrees with the ancient truth, "and faith once given," as St. Jude says, verse 3, it runs through all ages; and that wherein we agree with them is more agreeable and catholic than that they hold severed from us. It is more catholic in regard of all times, before Christ, and in Christ's time, and in the apostles' times; and that that the papists themselves hold with us, is more catholic than that they hold severed. Now wherein they differ from us, and we account them heretics, they differ from the

---

1 The commonplaces of the popish controversy. Consult Faber's "Difficulties of Romanism."—G.

Scriptures, and from the church six hundred years after Christ; and many of them are of late standing. Therefore in those tenets of ours we agree with the papists, and with the primitive church. What do we hold but they hold? But they add traditions that are pernicious. We hold the Scriptures. They hold that, and traditions too. We hold two sacraments. They add five more. We hold Christ to be the Mediator. They make saints mediators too. Whatsoever we hold they hold, but they add their own patcheries[1] to them. Therefore our doctrine is more catholic, because we have the evidence of Scripture for all ours, and we have them to justify ours; and wherein they differ from us, they have neither Scripture nor antiquity; but they are only a company, a mass of things of their own. But I will not be much in this point. And then, say they, where was your church before Luther's time, and two hundred years ago? Where was it? Where their church was. Our church was amongst them, in the midst of them. Witness their fire and inquisition, and persecution! They found out our church well enough.

But to make it a little clearer. The church of God, take it in general for good and bad in it, and for the means of salvation that they had in some measure, it may be called a kind of visible church, though very corruptly; and so considered, our

1 That is, "patchwork."=additions.—G.

church, those that possessed our religion, was the best of that church in the declining times of it. As in a lump of gold that is not yet refined to bullion there is gold, and a great deal of earth: take it in the whole, we say it is gold; but when it is refined to bullion, we say it is gold severed. Now our church in the midst of popery was as gold in the midst of earth unrefined; that is, there were[1] many Romish Churches, and ours was in the midst of them, the temple in the midst of the court; that is, the true church in the visible church. There were a great company that held the tenets of the gospel, especially at the hours of death, that denied popery. But then there were some that were refined as bullion after, as the Waldenses,[2] that were a severed company of people, besides other holy men and women that grew up by hearing somewhat of Christ in their sermons, and somewhat in the sacrament. They left out that that was bad, and took that that was good. Besides the lump of gold, there was some refined gold, when popery was in its perfection; and those they termed Waldenses, and the like. There was always a company that held the truth against them. I am sorry to mention these things, in a point tending more to edification. Our churches therefore are refined churches, that is, gold singled out of the

---

1 Misprinted "was."—G.
2 Consult Stanley Faber's "Waldenses and Albigenses"— able and trustworthy.—G.

dross of popery. They are a corrupt, and our church a refined, a visible congregation.

Now to cut off these objections, to come nearer to ourselves, to make good our particular congregations, and to show that of necessity we ought to frequent them, and to take heed of all objections that the devil and the flesh may make to bring us out of love with our particular congregations, know therefore these three or four rules in a word.

FIRST, that there has been *a church from the beginning of the world, where God has been worshipped.* Christ is a King, and he must have a kingdom. To believe a catholic church is an article of our faith, and there cannot be an act without an object. I have faith, I believe a visible church, therefore there must be a church. So that there has been a church from the beginning of the world. It is an article of our faith.[1]

SECONDLY, the mark whereby this church is known *is especially the truth of God.* That is the seed of the church, the truth of God discovered by his Word and ordinance. To which is annexed the sacraments and ecclesiastical government; but the former most necessary. And these three were typified in the ark; for there was the law signifying the Word, and the pot of manna signifying the sacrament, and the rod to show the discipline. Those three were, as it were, types of the three marks of the church. But

1 Consult Pearson, and also John Smith, *in loc.*—G.

especially the Word. For that is the seed of the new birth. Whersoever the Word has been published, and there has been an order of teachers, and people submitting themselves, there is a church, though perhaps there might be some weakness in other regards. A man is a man though he want the ornaments of a man; and a city without walls is a city. Put case there might be some weakness in some things, yet as long as the vitals of the church remain it is a church.

The THIRD thing that I observe, to clear this point, to hasten to things of more edification, is this, *abuse takes not away the use*. A neglectful use or abuse takes not away the true use of things. Put case the Scripture be abused many ways, that the sacraments have many additions, that these things are not so pure; yet it takes not away the just use; for then we take away the cause of things. Then the conclusion of all is this, that of necessity, notwithstanding somewhat may be found fault with in all visible churches, some errors there may be; yet we ought to cleave to a visible church, because it has been always, and we ought to know it by these marks. If the Word of God be taught there, then of necessity we must cleave to it. "God added to the church such as should be saved,"[1] to the visible church. Those that are saved must be saved in submission to the visible church. But these things I list not[2] to

---

1 Acts 2:47.

2 That is, "choose not."—G.

be large in. This may give satisfaction.

USE 1. If this be so, that we ought to submit to the ordinance of God in the visible church, to come into the ark as it were (the visible church is called the ark), or else we must be drowned and perish, *what shall we think then of those that are cast out of the church by excommunication* (but that is for their good)? But their case is very ill, because they are cut off from the house and beauty of God. Their case is miserable. But it is worse with those that depart out of themselves, as apostates, etc. Some are cast out, some are apostates and go out. They fall away from the church of God to the Romish strumpet, to Babylon; being dazzled with the pomp of that church, not seeing the spiritual beauty of the ordinances of God with us. What think we of those that ought to join with visible congregations, that excommunicate themselves willingly, such as schismatics, and such profane separatists, that when they may, will not; partly because they will not have their consciences awaked, and partly because they will give liberty to the flesh to other things at that time. Some are cast out, and some go out, some excommunicate themselves. They are of the disposition of the devils, that will not be "tormented before their time."[1] They think they shall hear somewhat that will awake their conscience, and they are very unwilling to have conscience awaked, but they will

1 Matthew 8:29.

have all their torment at once. All these are in a woeful condition. If the gracious presence of God be in the church above all other places in the world (as we see David desired "to dwell in the house of God, that he might see the beauty of God") if there be a beauty in the divine ordinances, how miserable are those that are cast out, or that go out! that rent themselves from the church, or willingly excommunicate themselves like wild creatures? They are worse than Cain. He grieved when he was to depart the presence of God. He fell into a desperate temper. They are worse than he, that when they have the liberty of the ordinances of God, they go on in a wild licentious course, and neglect all means that God has sanctified to bring them to heaven.

Use 2. But to come nearer, to make an use of trial, *how shall we know whether we have benefit by, and whether we be truly in love with, the beauty of God's house or no, because many come hither?* As in Noah's ark there were beasts that were clean and unclean, so there are many that come to the visible congregations; they are in the church (as excrements are in the body), but they are not of it.

To know therefore whether we come to purpose, and heartily love the beauty of God in his ordinances, and comforts and graces, as David did here or no, we may know it easily, *for sight*, as I said before, *it works affection*. We may know by our affection whether we see the excellency of God or no in his ordinances. There is no sense that stirs up affection answerable to sight; the affection of love especially.

How shall we know that we love the ordinances of God?

That is an affection that of all others is least to be concealed. What we love we will boldly profess; we will joy and delight in it if we have it. You see how David joyed in the ordinance of God, how he danced before the ark. There was no joy that he had comparable. He preferred it before all other joy that he had whatsoever. It was a transcendent joy. And what we love and delight in we meditate much on. "Oh how I love thy law! my meditation is on it continually."[1] Our minds will run on it. Therefore we are exhorted to think of the Word of God, to have it before our eyes, to have it written before us in our courses, that we may meditate upon it at home and abroad. Moses he gave those helps. Where there is love there is meditation. Those that love the good things of God, their minds will be often on them.

Again, there will be *zeal for the holy things of God.* A man will not endure them to be disgraced, but he will have a good word to speak in the defense of God's ordinances, of holy things and religion. Those that suffer religion to be betrayed in the company of base carnal people, they have never seen the beauty of God's house; [they] that have not a word

1 Psalm 119:97.

to say. Those that have seen God's beauty, and felt the comfort of the delights of God's house, they are able to justify it against all opposers whatsoever, that there is good to be taken and done there, by their own experience, by the comfort they have felt. They will be able to tell others what "the Lord has done for their souls,"[1] and in their souls, what graces they have been strengthened in, what comfort they have felt. They can discover this, and can justify all the ordinances of God from their own experience. Do not we see daily under the ordinance of God by weak men, the blind see, the spiritually deaf hear, the spiritually dumb be able to speak, to pray to God; the dead, those that are dead in sin, they receive life. Do not all these justify the excellency of God's ordinance, which gives spiritual life, and spiritual senses? Those therefore that have been dead in former time in sinful courses, and have found the power of God's Spirit with his ordinances, they are able to justify it. Those that are not able to justify these things by some experience, they never felt any good by them. By these and the like evidences, we may try the truth of our affection, whether we have seen this beauty or no to purpose.

QUESTION. If we find that we have little comfort and strength by the Word of God, that we have not seen the beauty of it, what shall we do, what course shall we take?

1 Psalm 66:16.

ANSWER. *Wait still.* Wait still at the pool for the angel's stirring,[1] for God at length will discover his power by his Spirit; he will discover his goodness, if not at the first, yet at length. Therefore let us use all sanctified means. And know this for a rule, that God's Spirit is an excellent worker. He will only work by his own instruments.

2. And *come to the ordinances with a spirit of faith*, because they are God's ordinances. God will discover himself in some excellency or other; he will discover some comfort and grace, somewhat that is useful to our souls to build us up to eternal life. Let us come with a particular faith that he will do so. Faith must answer God's promise. God has promised, "where two or three are met together in his name, he will be in the midst of them." He has made a promise to bless all his ordinances. Therefore let our particular faith answer God's ordinances. Lord, I go to thy house to hear thy Word, to receive thy sacrament in thy fear, in reverence of thy majesty, and in a spirit of faith, I expect thee to make good thy own ordinance. This brings a marvellous efficacy with it. If we go with a particular faith, know that God will be as good as his Word. This course we must take to see the beauty of the Lord.

3. And then, as I said before, *often let our thoughts be upon these spiritual excellencies*. Let us balance and weigh things in our thoughts.

1 John 5:4.

Love comes from judgment, love comes from an esteem of things, of the goodness of things, and that comes from a right judgment. Let us therefore labor to have a right judgment of things to be as they are. Solomon was the wisest man, next to him that was God-man, that ever was, and he knew what spiritual things were, and what all other things in the world were, and what does he give? This is the whole man, "to fear God and keep his commandments."[1] And how does he commend wisdom in Proverbs 8:1, seq. All precious things are nothing in comparison of the wisdom of God's Word. But what says he of other things? He that had run through all things by experience, and thought to extract the quintessence of all that the creature could give, he says they were but "vanity and vexation of spirit,"[2] trust my experience. Therefore let us be able to lay in the balance the good that we get or may get by the blessed ordinances of God, with other things whatsoever. Oh the beauty and excellency of spiritual things, it is above all other beauty whatsoever! Alas! what is outward beauty? it is but a lump of well-colored earth.[3] What is gold, and all the luster of it? It is but earth refined. And what are all honors and goodly delights that way? It is but a puff of smoke, it is nothing; in one word, it is vanity, and experience proves this every day. Oh!

1 Ecclesiastes 12:13.
2 Ecclesiastes 1:2.
3 See note a, vol. I., p. 31.—G.

but the "Word of the Lord endureth for ever,"[1] that is, the comforts, and the privileges that we have by the Word of God, they endure for ever; and then more especially the comfort of them when outward comforts fail most, even upon our deathbed. When conscience is awakened then, and has presented to it the former life, and the guilt of many sins, what will comfort a man then? his goodly apparel, or his goodly feature, or his great place and honor? (Perhaps these will increase his grief as they have been instruments of sin.) Oh no; this will do him good. Such a comfort I heard in such a sermon; such good things I heard read, and such good things come to my mind; such experience I have of God's Spirit working at such and such a time; these will testify that God's Spirit went with his ordinance to fasten somewhat on my soul, and they will comfort when nothing else will.

Let us oft compare all other things with the beauty of God, and his ordinances, as if all were nothing to them. Thus holy Moses, he saw a beauty and a glory in the despised people of God that made brick; he saw they were the people that God set his delight on, and that the church of God was there. When he saw that, he despised all the glory of Pharaoh's court, and accounted the worst thing in religion, "the reproach and shame," better than all the pleasures of sin.[2] Beloved, the bitterest things

1 1 Peter 1:25.
2 Hebrews 11:23.

in the ordinance of God are better than any worldly thing. What is the bitterest thing in the ordinance of God? Reproofs! They are as precious balm. If the ordinance of God meet with our particular sins, and tell us, and discover to us what an enemy it is, that it will be the bane of our souls if we live in it, and it send us away to look to ourselves, this will be as a precious balm; our souls will come to be saved by it. And if for religion we suffer reproach and shame, it will be as a crown, as holy Moses accounted the reproach of Christ better than the treasures of Egypt.[1] If the worst and bitterest things in God's ordinance be so sweet, what are the best things of all? The comforts of religion. What is the peace of conscience and joy in the Holy Ghost, and eternal glory in heaven? What are the excellencies of religion, when the shame and disgrace are to be preferred before all other things whatsoever?

So blessed St. Paul, he weighed things after this fashion. He was an excellent man, and had excellent privileges to glory in. Oh but, says he, I account all "dung and dross" in comparison of the excellent knowledge of Christ that he had.[2] Our blessed Saviour, that was the most able of all to judge, he would have all "sold for the pearl," that is, for the field where the pearl is (e.), to buy that, to get the ordinances of God. He accounts him a wise man

1 Hebrews 11:26.
2 Philippians 3:8.

that will sell all for that. And when Martha and Mary entertained him, Mary sat at his feet to hear him expound the truth of God; "she chose the better part,"[1] says Christ. If we will believe him "in whom all the treasures of wisdom are," in his judgment, "Mary chose the better part"; "One thing is necessary," says he. He justified David's choice, "One thing have I desired"; and says Christ, "One thing is necessary." All things in comparison of that are not necessary; they may well enough be spared. Thus we see how we may come to love God in his ordinances, and to see the "beauty of holiness," the beauty of God in his sanctuary.

4. And because there are two things needful to see a beauty, *an object revealed, and a sight,* let us desire God *to reveal himself in his ordinances to us more and more, and desire him to give us spiritual eyes more and more to see him.* Sometimes he hides himself in his ordinances, that we cannot see the beauty of things. Let us therefore desire him to reveal himself, to take away that veil that is between us and holy things, and between us and grace, and comfort, that he would take away that spiritual veil, and reveal himself to us, and shine on us in Christ, that he would manifest his love to us, and give us spiritual eyes to see him.

Prayer is an excellent means before we come; and when we are there, and oft in attending on the

1 Luke 10:42.

ordinances, let us lift up our hearts to God to reveal his truths to us.

There are many veils between us and holy things. Let us desire God to take them all away—of error, and ignorance, and unbelief—and to shine so clearly to us by his Spirit, that we may see him more clearly. And objects have a special influence when they are clearly discerned. Now a man may more clearly see and feel God at peace with him by the Spirit, and clearly see and feel the comfort of forgiveness of sins, and of any promise that is unfolded; and it has a marvellous influence upon the affections, to comfort and to breed peace and joy. And that is one sign that we profit by the ordinance of God, when it is so with us; when we find an influence from the things, upon our daily prayers, to work peace and comfort, and spiritual strength against temptations and corruptions. All in the ordinance is by the power of the Spirit. Therefore we are to pray to God that he would join his Holy Spirit, that he would reveal his secrets to us, and with revelation work an influence into our souls, that there may be a distilling of grace and comfort through the ordinances to our souls. Prayer must accompany the ordinances; because the ordinance of itself is an empty thing unless the Spirit accompany it.

To stir us up a little to this, more and more to see the beauty of God in his ordinances, to see the glory of God, as the Scripture speaks—indeed God is not only delightful and beautiful, but glorious in his ordinances; and the ark is called the "glory of God,"[1] and the knowledge of God in Christ it is a glorious knowledge, and the gospel is called a "glorious gospel,"[2]—*this will only*[3] *make us truly glorious*. These things, they put a glory upon our souls. St. Paul calls it "the glorious grace."[4] What a glorious thing is it when, by the ordinance of God, a weak man shall have power against the strong devil, against all the "gates of hell,"[5] when a poor creature, "flesh and blood," by some virtue distilled through the ordinance by the Spirit of God, shall have such a strong faith in the promise of forgiveness of sins; such a faith in the promise that all such[6] turn to his good; that God is reconciled to him in Christ; that all the gates of hell shall not prevail over a weak soul. And what a glorious grace is it when, by the use and attendance upon the ordinance of God, a poor soul shall have strength over these corruptions and sins that others are slaves to, and cannot get the victory over, that when they see the spiritual beauty in God's ordinances, they grow out of taste with all other things that others are besotted with,

1 Exodus 40:34.
2 1 Timothy 1:11.
3 That is, "this only."—G.
4 Ephesians 1:6.
5 Matthew 16:18.
6 Qu. "shall?"—ED.

that are of more excellent natural parts than they, what a glory of grace is this! Therefore let us with all fear and reverence attend upon the ordinances of God, that God may be glorious in us by his Spirit, and strengthen us against Satan and our beloved corruptions.

2. *And let us know what our souls were made for.* What are our souls more for than to dwell in the meditation of the beauty of God? What are our souls made for, but for excellent things? and what is excellent but in God's ordinances? Is the soul made to study debates and jars between man and man in our particular callings? Is the soul made to get a little wealth, that we shall leave perhaps to an unthrifty generation after? Are our souls, that are the most excellent things under heaven (the world is not worth a soul; they are the price of the blood of the Son of God; in his judgment the world is not worth a soul), are they for these things? No. They are for union and communion with God in his ordinances, to grow in nearer communion with God by his Spirit, to have more knowledge and affection, more love and joy and delight in the best things daily. Our souls are for these things that will make us gracious here, and glorious for ever after in heaven.

It is a great deordination,[1] when we study and care only for earthly things, and have slight conceits

1 That is, "disordering,"= placing out of order.—G.

of those things that are incomparably the best things, in the judgment of God and of Christ himself, and of Solomon, and of all good men.

3. And the rather let us be stirred up to affect these things, *lest God depart from us*. The glory of God departed out [of] the temple before the destruction of Jerusalem,[1] so the glory of God, that is, a visible sign of his glory, it departs from a church; the beauty and excellency of God departs when we esteem them not. And if anything in the world make God to leave a church, as he left the Jews, and as he may leave any particular church (he will always have a catholic church in the world; but he is not tied to England or France, or any country), if anything move him to this, it is because there is not a prizing of the heavenly things we have; of the blessed liberty we have to meet God in his ordinances; that we have not a care to improve these ordinances, to get grace and comfort against the evil day. For however we esteem these things, God sets a high price on them; and if we do not, God will deprive us of them, or of the power and beauty of them. Therefore as we desire God to continue his ordinances, and his blessing, and power in his ordinances, let us improve them the best way to get grace and comfort. He has made a great progress in religion, that has gotten a high esteem and a sanctified judgment of the best things. Though perhaps

1 Ezekiel 11:23.

he find himself dull and dead, and complain of it, yet when God shines so far that he is able to approve, and to justify the best things, that they touch his affections so much, that the bent of his soul is that way, and he cannot be long without them, and he finds much comfort by them, though it be joined with much corruption, these things argue a good temper and frame of soul.

And of all other dispositions of soul, let us preserve that spiritual disposition of soul, whereby our soul is fitted to the things themselves. The things of God's Spirit are holy and excellent, when there is such a taste and relish wrought in the soul suitable to the things. There is a happy combination then. We may know there is a powerful work of the things upon the soul, for all grace wrought by the things of God, we may know it when the soul has a suitable relish of them, and longs after them, and delights in them, and improves them to the best; and such a soul never wants evidence of a good Christian. Ask a Christian what is the best evidence of salvation, and that you belong to God? "My sheep hear my voice,"[1] says Christ, "and as children new born, desire the sincere milk of the Word, that ye may grow thereby."[2] A man may know he is a true child of the church if he desire the sincere milk of the Word, to grow better and more

1 John 10:4.
2 1 Peter 2:2.

holy and comfortable. If he delight in the voice of God in the ministry, and so be affected to the truth and ordinances of God, it is a comfortable character of a good Christian. There are more hidden evidences sometimes, but this for an ordinary evidence is a good one and comfortable. David marvelously comforted himself with this. "Oh! how do I love thy law."[1] Oh! that we could say as he did, "Oh how do I love thy law, and love thy truth," that we could wonder at our own affections, that we could delight in this beauty of God, as David says here, "One thing have I desired of the Lord, and that will I seek after, that I may dwell in the house of the Lord all the days of my life, to behold the beauty of the Lord," etc.

FINIS.

ENDNOTES

(*a.*) (PAGE 30.)—"Babylon was so taken," etc. Consult Herodotus, I. 177, *seq.*, with the annotations and illustrations of Rawlinson, *in loc.*; also Xenophon, *Cyrop*. vii. 5. For very interesting explorations confirmatory of the fact cf. Rich, "Babylon and Persepolis;" Ainsworth, "Researches in Assyria;" and Chesney, "Exped. for Survey of Euphrates." It need hardly be stated that it was Cyrus who took Babylon in the manner referred to by Sibbes.

---

1 Psalm 119:97.

(*b.*) (Page 54.)—"Particular visible churches are now God's tabernacle." In a tract by Philip Nye, entitled "The Lawfulness of the Oath of Supremacy, and Power of the King in Ecclesiastical Affairs" (4to, 1683, p. 41), the above and other context is quoted. On the margin is placed "Gospel Anointings," which misled us into inquiring after such a book (of which none had ever heard) by Sibbes. Another tractate, by Bartlet, his "Model of the Primitive Congregational Way" (4to, 1647), explains the mistake of Nye. The following was evidently his authority:—"I shall produce only one more that was famous for his *Gospell-anointings* [in italics, the usual mode of expressing quotations], and little thought by most men to have been of this judgment [in the margin here, 'see D. Sibbs']. And yet you shall find in a little treatise of his (printed before these troubles brake forth in England), called *A Breathing after God*, that he speaks fully to this purpose, his subject leading him to discover himself herein, being, as I suppose, a little before his death." Bartlet then quotes the passages to which the present note refers. The manner in which Nye was led into his mistake is quite apparent on an examination of Bartlet's tractate. Sibbes's name in the margin is exactly opposite the words "his *Gospell Anointings*," while the title of the book actually quoted does not appear till several lines lower on the page.

(*c.*) (Page 64.)—"As I have showed out of

that text, 2 Corinthians 3:18," etc. The sermons here referred to comprise the second half of Sibbes's "Excellency of the Gospel above the Law." 18mo, 1639.

(*d.*) (PAGE 92.)—"Where was your church before Luther?" etc. There have been many polemical answers to this taunting question. For *thoroughness* none perhaps excels the old Scottish tractate by Andrew Logie, "Answer to the question, Where was your religion before Luther?" Aberdeen, 1634, 4to.

(*e.*) (PAGE 104.)—"The field where the pearl is." Either Sibbes uses pearl as=treasure, or here, and elsewhere, he makes a slip. It is "treasure," not a "pearl," that is hidden in the "field." Matthew 13:44.—G.

Made in the USA
Monee, IL
21 June 2023